The Complete Off a Foodi Cookbook for Beginners

130 Delicious, Healthy, Quick & Easy-to-Prepare Recipes for You and Your Family

Table of Contents

Introduction 8

Chapter 1. Breakfast and Brunch 9

Onion And Scrambled Tofu 9
Breakfast Broccoli Casserole 10
Tantalizing Beef Jerky 11
Beefed Up Spaghetti Squash 12
Adobo Cubed Steak 13
Cool Beef Bourguignon 14
Philly Willy Steak And Cheese 15
Beef Stew 16
Bacon Strips 17
Quick Picadillo Dish 18
Breakfast Hash 19
Banana Bread 20
Polenta Balls 20
Oatmeal Casserole 21
Tomato Toast 22
Breakfast Hasbrown Casserole 23
Almond Butter Toast 24
Quinoa Pudding 25
Aromatic Meatballs 26
Generous Shepherd's Pie 27
Creamy Early Morning Asparagus Soup 28
Good-Day Pumpkin Puree 29

Chapter 2. Vegan and Vegetable 30

Cheese Dredged Cauliflower Delight 30
Garlic And Dill Carrot Fiesta 31
Cool Indian Palak Paneer 32
Astounding Caramelized Onions 33
Special Lunch-Worthy Green Beans 34
Healthy Cauliflower Mash 35

- Crispy Ratatouille Recipe 36
- Fully Stuffed Whole Chicken 38
- Rosemary Dredged Green Beans 39
- Italian Turkey Breast 40
- Crazy Fresh Onion Soup 41
- Smooth Carrots with Pancetta 42
- Chickpeas Masala 43
- Quinoa And Potato Salad 44
- Summertime Veggie Soup 45
- Delicious Mushroom Stroganoff 46
- Everyday Use Veggie-Stock 47
- Broccoli Florets 48
- Cauliflower And Cheddar Soup 49
- Butternut Squash Soup 50
- Cauliflower Gratin 51
- Zucchini Fries 52

Chapter 3. Fish and Seafood 53
- Buttered Up Scallops 53
- Awesome Cherry Tomato Mackerel 54
- Lovely Air Fried Scallops 55
- Packets Of Lemon And Dill Cod 56
- Adventurous Sweet And Sour Fish 57
- Cool Shrimp Zoodles 58
- Heartfelt Sesame Fish 59
- Awesome Sock-Eye Salmon 60
- Buttered Up Scallops 61
- Cherry Tomato Mackerel 62
- Garlic And Lemon Prawn Delight 63
- Lovely Carb Soup 64
- The Rich Guy Lobster And Butter 65
- Lovely Panko Cod 66
- Salmon Paprika 67
- Heartfelt Air Fried Scampi 68
- Ranch Warm Fillets 69
- Orange Sauce And Salmon 70

Cucumber And Salmon Mix 71

Chapter 4. Poultry and Meat 72

Mexican Beef Dish 72
All-Tim Favorite Beef Chili 73
Ingenious Bo Kho 74
Sesame Beef Ribs 75
The Chipotle Copycat Dish 76
All-Buttered Up Beef 77
Bruschetta Chicken Meal 78
The Great Hainanese Chicken 79
A Genuine Hassel Back Chicken 80
Shredded Up Salsa Chicken 81
Mexico's Favorite Chicken Soup 82
Taiwanese Chicken Delight 83
Beef And Broccoli Delight 84
Rich Beef Rendang 85
Spiritual Indian Beef Dish 86
Shredded Up Salsa Chicken 87
Mexico's Favorite Chicken Soup 88
Taiwanese Chicken Delight 89
Cabbage And Chicken Meatballs 90
Poached Chicken With Coconut Lime Cream Sauce 91
Hot And Spicy Paprika Chicken 92

Chapter 5. Beef Lamb and Pork 93

Fried Meatballs with Tomato Sauce 93
Keto Baked Beef Brisket 94
Pork Chops in Honey Mustard Sauce 95
Air Fried Pork Chops 96
Keto Garlic Butter Pork 97
Mediterranean Lamb Roast 98
Rosemary Lamb Chops 99
Pork Carnitas 100
Beef Pot Roast 101
Bone-In Pork Chops with Veggies 102

Pressure Cooked Adobo 103
Tex-Mex Meatloaf Recipe 104
Lamb and Eggplant Casserole 106
Beef Bites 108
Beef Chili & Cornbread Casserole 109
Pressure Cooked Short Ribs 111
Mexican Pork in Annatto Sauce 112
Red Wine Braised Short Ribs 113
Keto Corned Beef 114
Keto Steamed Pork 115

Chapter 6. Snacks and Appetizers 116

Kale And Almonds Mix 116
Simple Treat Of Garlic 117
Buttered Up Garlic And Fennel 118
Delicious Paprika And Cabbage 119
Authentic Western Omelet 120
Bowl Full Of Broccoli Salad 121
Rise And Shine Casserole 122
Cauliflower And Egg Dish 123
Just A Simple Egg Frittata 124
Ultimate Cheese Dredged Cauliflower Snack 125
Quick Turkey Cutlets 126
Veggies Dredged In Cheese 127
The Original Zucchini Gratin 128
Quick Bite Zucchini Fries 129
Pickled Up Green Chili 130
Egg Dredged Casserole 131
Excellent Bacon And Cheddar Frittata 132

Chapter 7. Holiday And Weekend Ninja Foodie Recipes 133

Simple Weeknight Vanilla Yogurt 133
The Great Family Lemon Mousse 134
Tangy Berry Slices 135
Over The Weekend Apple And Sprouts 136
Generous Gluten Free Pancakes 137

Fancy Holiday Lemon Custard 138
Gentle Peanut Butter Cheesecake 139
Decisive Crème Brulee 140
The Cool Pot-De-Crème 141
Humming Key Lime Curd 142
Runny Eggs In A Cup 143
Simple Party Week Poached Pears 144
Delicious Coconut Cake 145
Uniform Dark Chocolate Cake 146

Chapter 8. Side Dish 147

Carrot Fries 147
Brussels Sprouts 148
Asian Style Chickpeas 149
Bacon and Brussels Sprouts 150
Sweet Potato Mash 151
Oregano Potatoes 152
Carrot Puree 153
Baked Mushrooms 154
Roasted Potatoes 155
Cauliflower Risotto 156
Paprika Beets 157
Creamy Artichokes 158
Broccoli Mash 159
Cumin Green Beans 160
Lemony Carrots 161
Cauliflower Mix 162
Potato Salad 163
Zucchini Spaghetti 164
Garlicky Broccoli 165

Chapter 9. Desserts 166

Strawberry Cake 166
Balsamic Roasted Strawberries 167
Almond Cake 168
Creative Almond And Carrot Cake 169

Key Lime Curd	170
Chocolate Cheese Cake	171
Lemon Ricotta Cake	172
Lemon Mousse	173
Tangy Berry Slices	174
Almond Cheese Cake	175
Cinnamon Pears	176
Apple Bread	177
Apple Pudding	178
Easy Cake	179
Blackberries Cream	180
Graham Cheesecake	181
Raspberry Mug Cake	182
Strawberry Chocolate Chip Mug Cake	183
Chocolate Mug Cake	184
Coconut Cake	185
Carrot Pecan	186
Chapter 10. Grocery List	**187**
Frequently Asked Questions	191
Measurement Conversion Table	193
Chapter 11. 28 DAY MEAL-PLAN	**194**
1st Week Meal Plan	194
2nd Week Meal Plan	195
3rd Week Meal Plan	196
4Th Week Meal Plan	197
Chapter 12. Conclusion	**198**

Introduction

Ninja Foodi delivers a whole new way of cooking by providing a super combination of power, speed, and technology. It offers wholesome meals with great texture and flavor prepared from real foods. It's time to stop settling for convenience with delicious meals. Pressure cooking has been in practice for decades; we all are fond of our grandma's favorite recipes that have been invented using classic stovetop pressure cookers. Ninja Foodi multi-cookers and pressure cookers are just the same but with advanced features for ease of cooking.

Ninja Foodi is also popularly known as "one-pot wonder" for providing multiple cooking functions to cook a wide range of foods without using any additional unit but its core cooking pot.

- Multi-cookers

Multi-cookers models are available in 8-quarts and 6.5-quarts. Being a multi-cooker, it combines two functions of pressure cooking and Air Crisp technology for air frying. It acts as both a pressure cooker and an air fryer as it comes with two lids (Pressure Lid and Crisping Lid). Moreover, it also acts as a slow-cooker with slow cooking function.

- Pressure Cooking

Ninja Foodi pressure cookers include all the features and functions of multi-cooker except Air Crisp technology. Pressure cooker models are available in 8-quarts, 6.5-quarts, and 5-quartz.

It allows you to cook all types of pressure cooking and slow cooking cuisines. It comes with only Pressure Lid. However, some advanced models are offering

- Air Frying & Crisping

Air Fryers are, as the name suggests, for preparing crispy foods using Air Crisp technology. It comes with only Crisping Lid.

Breakfast and Brunch

Onion And Scrambled Tofu

Preparation Time: 8 minutes
Cooking Time: 12 minutes
Servings: 4
Ingredients:
- 4 tablespoons butter
- 2 tofu blocks, pressed and cubed in to 1 inch pieces
- Salt and pepper to taste
- 1 cup cheddar cheese, grated
- 2 medium onions, sliced

Directions:
1. Take a bowl and add tofu, season with salt and pepper
2. Set your Foodi to Saute mode and add butter , let it melt
3. Add onions and Saute for 3 minutes
4. Add seasoned tofu and cook for 2 minutes more
5. Add cheddar and gently stir
6. Lock the lid and bring down the Air Crisp mode, let the dish cook on "Air Crisp" mode for 3 minutes at 340 degrees F
7. Once done, take the dish out, serve and enjoy!

Nutrition Values (Per Serving):
Calories: 184
Fat: 12g
Carbohydrates: 5g
Protein: 12g

Breakfast Broccoli Casserole

Preparation Time: 10 minutes
Cooking Time: 7 minutes
Servings: 4
Ingredients:
1 tablespoon extra-virgin olive oil
1 pound broccoli, cut into florets
1 pound cauliflower, cut into florets
¼ cup almond flour
2 cups coconut milk
½ teaspoon ground nutmeg
Pinch of pepper
1 and ½ cup shredded Gouda cheese, divided
Directions:
Pre-heat your Ninja Foodi by setting it to Saute mode
Add olive oil and let it heat up, add broccoli and cauliflower
Take a medium bowl stir in almond flour, coconut milk, nutmeg, pepper, 1 cup cheese and add the mixture to your Ninja Foodi
Top with ½ cup cheese and lock lid, cook on HIGH pressure for 5 minutes
Release pressure naturally over 10 minutes
Serve and enjoy!
Nutrition Values (Per Serving):

Calories: 373

Fat: 32g
Carbohydrates: 6g
Protein: 16g

Tantalizing Beef Jerky

Preparation Time: 5 minutes
Cooking Time: 10 minutes
Servings: 2
Ingredients:
½ pound beef, sliced into 1/8 inch thick strips
½ cup of soy sauce
2 tablespoons Worcestershire sauce
2 teaspoons ground black pepper
1 teaspoon onion powder
½ teaspoon garlic powder
1 teaspoon salt
Directions:
Add listed ingredient to a large-sized Ziploc bag, seal it shut
Shake well, leave it in the fridge overnight
Lay strips on dehydrator trays, making sure not to overlap them
Lock Air Crisping Lid and set the temperature to 135 degrees F, cook for 7 hours
Store in airtight container, enjoy!
Nutrition Values (Per Serving):

Calories: 62
Fat: 7g
Carbohydrates: 2g
Protein: 9g

Beefed Up Spaghetti Squash

Preparation Time: 5 minutes
Cooking Time: 10 minutes
Servings: 4
Ingredients:
2 pounds ground beef
1 medium spaghetti squash
32 ounces marinara sauce
3 tablespoons olive oil
Directions:
Slice squash in half lengthwise and dispose of seeds
Add trivet to your Ninja Foodi
Add 1 cup water
Arrange squash on the rack and lock lid, cook on HIGH pressure for 8 minutes
Quick release pressure
Remove from pot
Clean pot and set your Ninja Foodi to Saute mode
Add ground beef and add olive oil, let it heat up
Add ground beef and cook until slightly browned and cooked
Separate strands from cooked squash and transfer to a bowl
Add cooked beef, and mix with marinara sauce
Serve and enjoy!
Nutrition Values (Per Serving):

Calories: 174
Fat: 6g
Carbohydrates: 5g
Protein: 19g

Adobo Cubed Steak

Preparation Time: 5 minutes
Cooking Time: 25 minutes
Servings: 4
Ingredients:
2 cups of water
8 steaks, cubed, 28 ounces pack
Pepper to taste
1 and ¾ teaspoons adobo seasoning
1 can (8 ounces) tomato sauce
1/3 cup green pitted olives
2 tablespoons brine
1 small red pepper
½ a medium onion, sliced
Directions:
Chop peppers, onions into ¼ inch strips
Prepare beef by seasoning with adobo and pepper
Add into Ninja Foodi
Add remaining ingredients and Lock lid, cook on HIGH pressure for 25 minutes
Release pressure naturally
Serve and enjoy!
Nutrition Values (Per Serving):

Calories: 154
Fat: 5g
Carbohydrates: 3g
Protein: 23g

Cool Beef Bourguignon

Preparation Time: 10 minutes
Cooking Time: 30 minutes
Servings: 4
Ingredients:
1 pound stewing steak
½ pound bacon
5 medium carrots, diced
1 large red onion, peeled and sliced
2 garlic cloves, minced
2 teaspoons salt
2 tablespoons fresh thyme
2 tablespoons fresh parsley
2 teaspoons ground pepper
½ cup beef broth
1 tablespoon olive oil
1 tablespoon sugar-free maple syrup (Keto friendly)
Directions:
Set your Ninja Foodi to Saute mode and add 1 tablespoon of oil, allow the oil to heat up
Pat your beef dry and season it well
Add beef into the Ninja Foodi (in batches) and Saute them until nicely browned up
Slice up the cooked bacon into strips and add the strips to the pot
Add onions as well and brown them
Add the rest of the listed ingredients and lock up the lid
Cook for 30 minutes on HIGH pressure
Allow the pressure to release naturally over 10 minutes
Enjoy!
Nutrition Values (Per Serving):

Calories: 416
Fats: 18g
Carbs: 12g
Protein:27g

Philly Willy Steak And Cheese

Preparation Time: 10 minutes
Cooking Time: 40 minutes
Servings: 4
Ingredients:
2 tablespoons olive oil
2 large onion, sliced
8 ounces mushrooms, sliced
1-2 teaspoons Keto friendly steak seasoning
1 tablespoon butter
2 pounds beef chuck roast
12 cup beef stock
Directions:

Set your Ninja Foodi to Saute mode and add oil, let it heat up
Rub seasoning over roast and Saute for 1-2 minutes per side
Remove and add butter, onion
Add mushrooms, pepper, stock, and roast
Lock lid and cook on HIGH pressure for 35 minutes
Naturally, release pressure over 10 minutes
Shred meat and sprinkle cheese if using, enjoy!
Nutrition Values (Per Serving):

Calories: 425
Fats: 25g
Carbs: 3g
Protein: 46g

Beef Stew

Preparation Time: 10 minutes
Cooking Time: 10 minutes
Servings: 4
Ingredients:
1 pound beef roast
4 cups beef broth
3 garlic cloves, chopped
1 carrot, chopped
2 celery stalks, chopped
2 tomatoes, chopped
½ white onion, chopped
¼ teaspoon salt
1/8 teaspoon ground black pepper
Directions:

Add listed ingredients to your Ninja Foodi and lock lid, cook on HIGH pressure for 10 minutes
Quick release pressure
Open the lid and shred the bee using forks, serve and enjoy!
Nutrition Values (Per Serving):
Calories: 211
Fat: 7g
Carbohydrates: 2g
Protein: 10g

Bacon Strips

Preparation Time: 5 minutes
Cooking Time: 7 minutes
Servings: 2
Ingredients:
10 bacon strips
¼ teaspoon chili flakes
1/3 teaspoon salt
¼ teaspoon basil, dried
Directions:
Rub the bacon strips with chili flakes, dried basil, and salt
Turn on your air fryer and place the bacon on the rack
Lower the air fryer lid
Cook the bacon at 400F for 5 minutes
Cook for 3 minutes more if the bacon is not fully cooked
Serve and enjoy!
Nutrition Values (Per Serving):
Calories: 500
Fat: 46g
Carbohydrates: 0g
Protein: 21g

Quick Picadillo Dish

Preparation Time: 10 minutes
Cooking Time: 15 minutes
Servings: 4
Ingredients:
½ pound lean ground beef
2 garlic cloves, minced
½ large onion, chopped
1 teaspoon salt
1 tomato, chopped
½ red bell pepper, chopped
1 tablespoon cilantro
½ can (4 ounces) tomato sauce
1 teaspoon ground cumin
1-2 bay leaves
2 tablespoons green olives, capers
2 tablespoons brine
3 tablespoons water
Directions:
Set your Ninja Foodi to Saute mode and add meat, salt, and pepper, slightly brown
Add garlic, tomato, onion, cilantro and Saute for 1 minute
Add olives, brine, leaf, cumin, and mix
Pour in sauce, water, and stir
Lock lid and cook on HIGH pressure for 15 minutes
Quick release pressure
Nutrition Values (Per Serving):
Calories: 207
Fats: 8g
Carbs: 4g
Protein: 25g

Breakfast Hash

Preparation Time: 5 minutes
Cooking Time: 5 minutes
Servings: 2
Ingredients:
½ cup sweet potatoes, peeled, cut in 1/2-inch pieces
1/8 cup precooked Spanish chorizo, cut in 1/2-inch pieces
½ small onion, peeled, cut in 1/2-inch pieces
¼ cup mixed vegetables like carrots, green beans, corn
1 tablespoon avocado oil
½ teaspoon paprika
½ teaspoon salt
Directions:
Place Sweet potatoes, Spanish chorizo, onion, and frozen vegetables in a large bowl. Add avocado, paprika and salt. Toss Ingredients to coat.
Place Ingredients on Ninja Sheet Pan, spreading out evenly.
Select BAKE, set temperature to 400°F, and set time to 20 minutes. Press START/PAUSE to begin preheating.
When unit has preheated, place pan in oven. After 10 minutes, remove pan and mix Ingredients with a wooden spoon or spatula. Return pan to oven and cook for 10 more minutes.
When cooking is complete, remove pan from oven and cool for 5 minutes before serving.
Nutrition Values (Per Serving):
Calories: 120
Fats: 4g
Carbs: 6g
Protein: 18g

Banana Bread

Preparation Time: 15 minutes
Cooking Time: 40 minutes
Servings: 2
Ingredients:
2 cups coconut flour
1 teaspoon baking soda
1/4 teaspoon kosher salt
2 tablespoon coconut oil
¼ cup maple syrup
2 eggs, beaten
3 medium ripe bananas, mashed

Directions:
Close crisping lid. Preheat the unit by selecting BAKE/ROAST, setting the temperature to 325°F, and setting the time to 5 minutes. Select START/STOP to begin.
Meanwhile, in a bowl, stir together coconut flour, baking soda, and salt.
In a separate bowl, beat together coconut oil and maple syrup. Add eggs and bananas and stir to combine.
Slowly add dry mixture to wet mixture, stirring until just combined.
Grease the Ninja loaf pan (or an 8-inch baking pan):and add batter to pan.
Once unit has preheated, place pan on reversible rack, making sure rack is in the lower position. Close crisping lid. Select BAKE/ROAST, set temperature to 325°F, and set time to 40 minutes. Select START/STOP to begin.
When cooking is complete, remove pan from pot and place on a cooling rack. Allow bread to cool 30 minutes before serving.

Nutrition Values (Per Serving):
Calories: 545
Fats: 7g
Carbs: 9g
Protein: 20g

Oatmeal Casserole

Preparation Time: 10 minutes
Cooking Time: 30 minutes
Servings: 6
Ingredients:
1 banana, peeled and mashed
2 cups milk
2 eggs; whisked.
2 cups old fashioned oats
1/3 cup sugar
1 cup blueberries
2 tbsp. butter
1 tsp. cinnamon powder
1 tsp. baking powder
1 tsp. vanilla extract
Cooking spray

Directions:

In a bowl mix the sugar with baking powder, cinnamon, blueberries, banana, milk, eggs, butter, vanilla and whisk. Grease the Foodi's baking dish with cooking spray, add oats on the bottom, add the berries and banana mix and toss

Put the reversible rack in the machines, put the baking dish inside, put the pressure lid on, seal and cook on High for 20 minutes. Release the pressure naturally for 10 minutes, divide into bowls and serve for breakfast.

Nutrition Values (Per Serving):
Calories: 550
Fats: 8g
Carbs: 4g
Protein: 25g

Tomato Toast

Preparation Time: 10 minutes
Cooking Time: 11 minutes
Servings: 3
Ingredients:
6 bread slices
3 garlic cloves; minced.
1 cup mozzarella cheese; grated.
5 tbsp. butter, melted
6 tsp. tomato pesto
Directions:
Arrange bread slices on a working surface, spread the butter and all the other ingredients on each.
Add the basket in the Foodi machine, add the bread slices inside, set the pot on Air Crisp and cook everything for 8 minutes at 350 °F. Divide the toast between plates and serve
Nutrition Values (Per Serving):
Calories: 543
Fats: 9g
Carbs: 3g
Protein: 18g

Breakfast Hasbrown Casserole

Preparation Time: 15 minutes
Cooking Time: 40 minutes
Servings: 10
Ingredients:
1 lb. ham; chopped.
48 oz. hash browns
½ cup cheddar cheese, shredded
1 yellow onion; chopped.
¼ cup milk
6 eggs; whisked.
3 tbsp. olive oil
Directions:
Set your Foodi on sauté mode, add the oil, heat it up, add the onion, stir and cook for 3-4 minutes.
Add hash browns and the ham, set the Foodi on Air Crisp and cook for 15 minutes, stirring everything halfway
Add eggs mixed with hash browns and cook everything on Air Crisp for 10 minutes more. Sprinkle the cheese on top, divide everything between plates and serve for breakfast
Nutrition Values (Per Serving):
Calories: 197
Fats: 10g
Carbs: 4g
Protein: 18g

Almond Butter Toast

Preparation Time: 10 minutes
Cooking Time: 0 minutes
Servings: 2
Ingredients:
2 slices Tempeh, cooked, cooled
2 tablespoons almond butter
½ tablespoon tomato sauce
½ tablespoon fresh lime juice
1/8 teaspoon salt
1/8 teaspoon ground pepper
2 slices browned bread, toasted
Directions:
Place the Total Crushing & Power Chopping Blade into the Jar, then add cooked Tempeh. Pulse 3 times, then transfer chopped bacon to a small bowl.
Add almond butter, tomato sauce, lime juice, salt, and pepper to the jar. Pulse 7 times, then run continuously for 20 seconds.
Top each slice of toasted bread with approximately 2 tablespoons almond butter spread and chopped tempeh.
Nutrition Values (Per Serving):
Calories: 210
Fats: 10g
Carbs: 4g
Protein: 10g

Quinoa Pudding

Preparation Time: 5 minutes
Cooking Time: 5 minutes
Servings: 2
Ingredients:
½ cup quinoa
2 cups coconut milk, cold, divided
1/8 cup maple syrup
2 strips lime zest
1 cinnamon sticks
1/8 teaspoon kosher salt
1/2 cup heavy cream
Ground nutmeg, for garnish
Directions:
Place quinoa, 1-1/2 cups coconut milk, maple syrup, lime zest, cinnamon sticks, and salt into the pot. Stir to combine.
Assemble pressure lid, making sure the pressure release valve is in the SEAL position. Select PRESSURE and set to HIGH. Set time to 2 minutes. Select START/STOP to begin.
When pressure cooking is complete, allow pressure to release naturally for 10 minutes. After 10 minutes, quick release any remaining pressure by moving the pressure release valve to the VENT position. Carefully remove lid when unit has finished releasing pressure.
Add heavy cream to the pot and stir to incorporate.
Select SEAR/SAUTÉ and set to MED. Select START/STOP to begin. Allow to simmer for 5 minutes, stirring frequently.
Carefully remove pot to a heat-safe surface. Stir in the remaining milk and allow to cool for 15 minutes.
Serve warm after 15 minutes, or cool to room temperature then refrigerate and serve cold, garnished with ground nutmeg
Nutrition Values (Per Serving):
Calories: 543
Fats: 21g
Carbs: 16g
Protein: 9g

Aromatic Meatballs

Preparation Time: 8 minutes
Cooking Time: 11 minutes
Servings: 4
Ingredients
2 cups ground beef
1 egg, beaten
1 teaspoon Taco seasoning
1 tablespoon sugar-free marinara sauce
1 teaspoon garlic, minced
½ teaspoon salt
Directions:
Take a big mixing bowl and place all the ingredients into the bowl
Add all the ingredients into the bowl
Mix together all the ingredients by using a spoon or fingertips
Then make the small size meatballs and put them in a layer in the air fryer rack
Lower the air fryer lid
Cook the meatballs for 11 minutes at 350 F
Serve immediately and enjoy!
Nutrition Values (Per Serving):
Calories: 205
Fat: 12.2g
Carbohydrates: 2.2g
Protein: 19.4g

Generous Shepherd's Pie

Preparation Time: 10 minutes
Cooking Time: 15 minutes
Servings: 4
Ingredients

2 cups of water
4 tablespoons butter
4 ounces cream cheese
1 cup mozzarella
1 whole egg
Salt and pepper to taste
1 tablespoon garlic powder
2-3 pounds ground beef
1 cup frozen carrots
8 ounces mushrooms, sliced
1 cup beef broth

Directions:

Add water to Ninja Foodi, arrange cauliflower on top, lock lid and cook for 5 minutes on HIGH pressure
Quick release and transfer to a blender, add cream cheese, butter, mozzarella cheese, egg, pepper, and salt. Blend well
Drain water from Ninja Foodi and add beef
Add carrots, garlic powder, broth and pepper, and salt
Add in cauliflower mix and lock lid, cook for 10 minutes on HIGH pressure
Release pressure naturally over 10 minutes
Serve and enjoy!

Nutrition Values (Per Serving):

Calories: 303
Fats: 21g
Carbs: 4g
Protein: 21g

Creamy Early Morning Asparagus Soup

Preparation Time: 10 minutes
Cooking Time: 10 minutes
Servings: 2
Ingredients

1 tablespoon olive oil
3 green onions, sliced crosswise into ¼ inch pieces
1 pound asparagus, tough ends removed, cut into 1 inch pieces
4 cups vegetable stock
1 tablespoon unsalted butter
1 tablespoon almond flour
2 teaspoon salt
1 teaspoon white pepper
½ cup heavy cream

Directions:

Set your Ninja Foodi to "Saute" mode and add oil, let it heat up
Add green onions and Saute for a few minutes, add asparagus and stock
Lock lid and cook on HIGH pressure for 5 minutes
Take a small saucepan and place it over low heat, add butter, flour and stir until the mixture foams and turns into a golden beige, this is your blond roux
Remove from heat
Release pressure naturally over 10 minutes
Open lid and add roux, salt and pepper to the soup
Use an immersion blender to puree the soup
Taste and season accordingly, swirl in cream and enjoy!

Nutrition Values (Per Serving):

Calories: 192
Fat: 14g
Carbohydrates: 8g
Protein: 6g

Good-Day Pumpkin Puree

Preparation Time: 10 minutes
Cooking Time: 15 minutes
Servings: 2
Ingredients

2 pounds small sized pumpkin, halved and seeded
½ cup water
Salt and pepper to taste
Directions:

Add water to your Ninja Foodi, place steamer rack in the pot
Add pumpkin halves to the rack and lock lid, cook on HIGH pressure for 13-15 minutes
Once done, quick release pressure and let the pumpkin cool
Once done, scoop out flesh into a bowl
Blend using an immersion blender and season with salt and pepper
Serve and enjoy!
Nutrition Values (Per Serving):
Calories: 112
Fat: 2g
Carbohydrates: 7g
Protein: 2g

Vegan and Vegetable

Cheese Dredged Cauliflower Delight

Preparation Time: 15 minutes
Cooking Time: 43 minutes
Servings: 2
Ingredients:
- 1 tablespoon Keto-Friendly mustard
- 1 head cauliflower
- 1 teaspoon avocado mayonnaise
- ½ cup parmesan cheese, grated
- ¼ cup butter, cut into small pieces

Directions:
Set your Ninja Foodi to Sauté mode and add butter, let it melt
Add cauliflower and Sauté for 3 minutes
Add remaining ingredients and lock lid
Cook on PRESSURE mode for 30 minutes on HIGH pressure
Release pressure natural over 10 minutes
Serve and enjoy!

Nutrition Values (Per Serving):
Calories: 478
Fats: 5g
Carbs: 8g
Protein: 18g

Garlic And Dill Carrot Fiesta

Preparation Time: 15 minutes
Cooking Time: 10 minutes
Servings: 4
Ingredients:
3 cups carrots, chopped
1 tablespoon melted butter
½ teaspoon garlic sea salt
1 tablespoon fresh dill, minced
1 cup water

Directions:
Add listed ingredients to Ninja Foodi
Stir and lock lid, cook on HIGH pressure for 10 minutes
Release pressure naturally over 10 minutes
Quick release pressure and remove lid
Serve with a topping of dill, enjoy!
Nutrition Values (Per Serving):
Calories: 207
Fats: 16g
Carbs: 5g
Protein: 8g

Cool Indian Palak Paneer

Preparation Time: 15 minutes
Cooking Time: 10 minutes
Servings: 4
Ingredients:
2 teaspoons olive oil
5 garlic cloves, chopped
1 tablespoon fresh ginger, chopped
1 large yellow onion, chopped
½ jalapeno chile, chopped
1 pound fresh spinach
2 tomatoes, chopped
2 teaspoons ground cumin
½ teaspoon cayenne
2 teaspoons Garam masala
1 teaspoon ground turmeric
1 teaspoon salt
½ cup water
1 and ½ cup paneer cubes
½ cup heavy whip cream

Directions:
Pre-heat your Ninja Foodi using Sauté mode on HIGH heat, once the pot is hot, add oil and let it shimmer
Add garlic, ginger and Chile, Sauté for 2-3 minutes
Add onion, spinach, tomatoes, cumin, cayenne, garam masala, turmeric, salt and water
Lock lid and cook on HIGH pressure for 2 minutes
Release pressure naturally over 10 minutes
Use an immersion blender to puree the mixture to your desired consistency
Gently stir in paneer and top with a drizzle of cream. Enjoy!

Nutrition Values (Per Serving):
Calories: 188
Fats: 14g
Carbs: 7g
Protein: 7g

Astounding Caramelized Onions

Preparation Time: 15 minutes
Cooking Time: 45 minutes
Servings: 4
Ingredients:
2 tablespoons unsalted butter
3 large onions, sliced
2 tablespoons water
1 teaspoon salt
Directions:
Set your pot to Sauté mode and adjust the heat to Medium, pre-heat the inner pot for 5 minutes
Add butter and let it melt, add onions, water, salt, and stir well
Lock pressure lid into place, making sure that the pressure valve is locked
Cook on HIGH pressure for 30 minutes
Quick release the pressure once done
Remove the lid and set the pot to Sauté mode, let it sear in the Medium-HIGH mode for about 15 minutes until the liquid is almost gone
Nutrition Values (Per Serving):
Calories: 110
Fats: 6g
Carbs: 10g
Protein: 15g

Special Lunch-Worthy Green Beans

Preparation Time: 5 minutes
Cooking Time: 5 minutes
Servings: 4
Ingredients:
2-3 pounds fresh green beans
2 tablespoons butter
1 garlic clove, minced
Salt and pepper to taste
1 and ½ cups water
Directions:
Add all listed ingredients to your Ninja Foodi pot
Lock lid and cook on HIGH pressure for 5 minutes
Release pressure quickly and serve

Nutrition Values (Per Serving):
Calories: 87
Fats: 5g
Carbs: 5g
Protein: 3g

Healthy Cauliflower Mash

Preparation Time: 5 minutes
Cooking Time: 15 minutes
Servings: 4
Ingredients:
1 tablespoon butter, soft
½ cup feta cheese
Salt and pepper to taste
1 large head cauliflower, chopped into large pieces
1 garlic cloves, minced
2 teaspoons fresh chives, minced

Directions:
Add the pot to your Ninja Foodi and add water
Add steamer basket on top and add cauliflower pieces
Lock lid and cook on HIGH pressure for 5 minutes
Quick release pressure
Open lid and use an immersion blender to mash the cauliflower
Blend until you have your desired consistency and enjoy!

Nutrition Values (Per Serving):
Calories: 358
Fats: 9g
Carbs: 10g
Protein: 15g

Crispy Ratatouille Recipe

Preparation Time: 5 minutes
Cooking Time: 10 minutes
Servings: 4
Ingredients:
1 14.5-ounce can diced tomatoes; undrained
1 small red bell pepper; cut into ½-inch chunks about 1 cup
1 small green bell pepper; cut into ½-inch chunks about 1 cup
1 rib celery; sliced about 1 cup
Kosher salt; for salting and seasoning
1 small eggplant; peeled and sliced 1/2-inch thick
1 medium zucchini; sliced 1/2-inch thick
2 tbsp. olive oil
1 cup chopped onion
3 garlic cloves; minced or pressed
1/2 tsp. dried oregano
1/4 tsp. freshly ground black pepper
2 tbsp. minced fresh basil
1/4 cup water
1/4 cup pitted green or black olives optional

Directions:
Place a rack on a baking sheet. With kosher salt, very liberally salt one side of the eggplant and zucchini slices and place them, salted-side down, on the rack. Salt the other side.
Let the slices sit for 15 to 20 minutes or until they start to exude water you'll see it beading up on the surface of the slices and dripping into the sheet pan. Rinse the slices and blot them dry. Cut the zucchini slices into quarters and the eggplant slices into eighths
Turn the Ninja Foodi Multi-cooker to *Sauté*, heat the olive oil until it shimmers and flows like water. Add the onion and garlic and sprinkle with a pinch or two of kosher salt. Cook for about 3 minutes, stirring until the onions just begin to brown
Add the eggplant, zucchini, green bell pepper, red bell pepper, celery and tomatoes with their juice, water and oregano
High pressure for 4 minutes. Lock the lid on the Ninja Foodi Multi-cooker and then cook for 4 minutes.
To get 4 minutes' cook time, press *Pressure* button and use the Time Adjustment button to adjust the cook time to 4 minutes
Pressure Release. Use the quick release method
Finish the dish. Unlock and remove the lid. Close the crisping lid. Select "BROIL" and set the time to 5 minutes. Select START/STOP to begin. Cook until top is browned

Stir in the pepper, basil and olives if using. Taste, adjust the seasoning as needed and serve.

While this vegetable dish is usually served on its own, it's great tossed with cooked pasta or served over polenta.

Nutrition Values (Per Serving):
Calories: 187
Fats: 8g
Carbs: 4g
Protein: 25g

Fully Stuffed Whole Chicken

Preparation Time: 5 minutes
Cooking Time: 8 hours 0 minutes
Servings: 2

Ingredients:

1 cup mozzarella cheese
4 garlic clove, peeled
1 whole chicken, 2 pounds, cleaned and dried
Salt and pepper to taste
2 tablespoons lemon juice

Directions:

Stuff chicken cavity with garlic cloves, cheese. Season with salt and pepper
Transfer to Ninja Foodi and drizzle lemon juice. Lock lid and SLOW COOK on LOW for 8 hours
Transfer to a plate, serve and enjoy!

Nutrition Values (Per Serving):

Calories: 309
Fat: 12g
Carbohydrates: 1.6g
Protein: 45g

Rosemary Dredged Green Beans

Preparation Time: 5 minutes
Cooking Time: 3 hours 0 minutes
Servings: 4

Ingredients

1 pound green beans
1 tablespoon rosemary, minced
1 teaspoon fresh thyme, minced
2 tablespoons lemon juice
2 tablespoons water

Directions:

Add listed ingredients to Ninja Foodi
Lock lid and cook on SLOW COOK MODE (LOW) for 3 hours. Unlock lid and stir. Enjoy!

Nutrition Values (Per Serving):

Calories: 40
Fat: 0g
Carbohydrates: 9g
Protein: 2g

Italian Turkey Breast

Preparation Time: 5 minutes
Cooking Time: 2 hours 0 minutes
Servings: 4

Ingredients

1 and ½ cups Italian dressing
2 garlic cloves, minced
1 (2 pounds) turkey breast, with bone
2 tablespoons butter
Salt and pepper to taste

Directions:

Mix in garlic cloves, salt, black pepper and rub turkey breast with mix
Grease Ninja Foodi pot and arrange turkey breast. Top with Italian dressing
Lock lid and BAKE/ROAST for 2 hours at 230 degrees F. Serve and enjoy!

Nutrition Values (Per Serving):

Calories: 369
Fat: 23g
Carbohydrates: 6g
Protein: 35g

Crazy Fresh Onion Soup

Preparation Time: 5 minutes
Cooking Time: 10 minutes
Servings: 4

Ingredients

2 tablespoons avocado oil
8 cups yellow onion
1 tablespoon balsamic vinegar
6 cups of pork stock
1 teaspoon salt
2 bay leaves
2 large sprigs, fresh thyme

Directions:

Cut up the onion in half through the root
Peel them and slice into thin half moons
Set the pot to Saute mode and add oil, one the oil is hot and add onions
Cook for about 15 minutes
Add balsamic vinegar and scrape any fond from the bottom
Add stock, bay leaves, salt, and thyme
Lock up the lid and cook on HIGH pressure for 10 minutes
Release the pressure naturally
Discard the bay leaf and thyme stems
Blend the soup using an immersion blender and serve!

Nutrition Values (Per Serving):

Calories: 454
Fat: 31g
Carbohydrates: 7g
Protein: 27g

Smooth Carrots with Pancetta

Preparation Time: 10 minutes
Cooking Time: 18 minutes
Servings: 4
Ingredients:
1 lb. baby carrots
4-ounces pancetta; diced
1/4 cup moderately sweet white wine; such as a dry Riesling
1 medium leek; white and pale green parts only, sliced lengthwise, washed and thinly sliced
1/2 tsp. ground black pepper
2 tbsp. unsalted butter; cut into small bits

Directions:
Put the pancetta in the Ninja Foodi turned to the *Air crisp* function and use the Time Adjustment button to adjust the cook time to 5 minutes
Add the leek; cook, often stirring, until softened. Pour in the wine and scrape up any browned bits at the bottom of the pot as it comes to a simmer
Add the carrots and pepper; stir well. Scrape and pour the contents of the Ninja Foodi Multi-cooker into a 1-quart, round, high-sided soufflé or baking dish.
Dot with the bits of butter. Lay a piece of parchment paper on top of the dish, then a piece of aluminum foil. Seal the foil tightly over the baking dish.
Set the Ninja Foodi Multi-cooker rack inside and pour in 2 cups water. Use aluminum foil to build a sling for the baking dish; lower the baking dish into the cooker.
High pressure for 7 minutes. Lock the lid on the Ninja Foodi Multi-cooker and then cook for 7 minutes.
To get 7 minutes' cook time, press *Pressure* button and use the Time Adjustment button to adjust the cook time to 7 minutes.
Pressure Release. Use the quick release method to return the pot's pressure to normal.
Finish the dish. Close the crisping lid. Select "BROIL" and set the time to 5 minutes.
Select START/STOP to begin. Cook until top is browned
Unlock and open the pot. Use the foil sling to lift the baking dish out of the cooker. Uncover, stir well and serve.

Nutrition Values (Per Serving):
Calories: 335
Fats: 9g
Carbs: 4g
Protein: 13g

Chickpeas Masala

Preparation Time: 15 minutes
Cooking Time: 1 hour 10 minutes
Servings: 8
Ingredients:
1 lb. chickpeas
28 oz. canned tomatoes; chopped.
14 oz. coconut milk
1 yellow onion; chopped.
A pinch of salt and black pepper
6 garlic cloves; minced.
1 bunch cilantro; chopped.
1 green chili pepper; chopped.
2 and ½ cups water
4 tbsp. coconut oil, melted
1 tbsp. ginger; grated.
1 tbsp. cumin, ground
1 tsp. chili powder
2 tsp. garam masala
2 tsp. sugar
1 tsp. turmeric powder
Juice of 2 lemons

Directions:
Set the Foodi machine on Sauté mode, add the oil, heat it up, add the onion, salt, pepper and the cumin, stir and sauté for 5 minutes
Add the turmeric, garlic, ginger, chili, chili powder and the cilantro, stir and sauté for 2 more minutes. Add the tomatoes, water, coconut milk and the chickpeas, toss, put the pressure lid on and cook on Low for 40 minutes
Release the pressure naturally for 10 minutes, add the sugar, garam masala and the lemon juice, toss, set the Foodi on Sauté mode again and cook everything for 5 more minutes. Divide everything into bowls and serve.

Nutrition Values (Per Serving):
Calories: 424
Fats: 8g
Carbs: 4g
Protein: 9g

Quinoa And Potato Salad

Preparation Time: 5 minutes
Cooking Time: 25 minutes
Servings: 4
Ingredients:
1 ½ lb. tiny white potatoes; halved
1/4 cup white balsamic vinegar
1 cup blond white quinoa
1 medium shallot; minced
2 medium celery stalks; thinly sliced
1 large dill pickle; diced
1 tbsp. Dijon mustard
1 tsp. sweet paprika
1/2 tsp. ground black pepper
1/4 tsp. celery seeds
1/4 tsp. salt
1/4 cup olive oil
Directions:
Whisk the vinegar, mustard, paprika, pepper, celery seeds and salt in a large serving bowl until smooth; whisk in the olive oil in a thin, steady stream until the dressing is fairly creamy.
Place the potatoes and quinoa in the Ninja Foodi Multi-cooker; add enough cold tap water so that the ingredients are submerged by 3 inches some of the quinoa may float High pressure for 10 minutes. Lock the lid on the Ninja Foodi Multi-cooker and then cook for 10 minutes.
To get 10 minutes' cook time, press *Pressure* button and use the Time Adjustment button to adjust the cook time to 10 minutes.
Pressure Release. Use the quick release method to bring the pot's pressure back to normal.
Finish the dish. Unlock and open the pot. Close the crisping lid. Select "BROIL" and set the time to 5 minutes. Select START/STOP to begin
Cook until top is browned. Drain the contents of the pot into a colander lined with paper towels or into a fine-mesh sieve in the sink. Do not rinse.
Transfer the potatoes and quinoa to the large bowl with the dressing. Add the shallot, celery and pickle; toss gently and set aside for a minute or two to warm up the vegetables
Nutrition Values (Per Serving):
Calories: 185
Fats: 4g
Carbs: 28g
Protein: 3g

Summertime Veggie Soup

Preparation Time: 5 minutes
Cooking Time: 10 minutes
Servings: 6
Ingredients:
3 cups leeks, sliced
6 cups rainbow chard, stems and leaves, chopped
1 cup celery, chopped
2 tablespoons garlic, minced
1 teaspoon dried oregano
1 teaspoon salt
2 teaspoons fresh ground black pepper
3 cups chicken broth
2 cups yellow summer squash, sliced into 1/ inch slices
¼ cup fresh parsley, chopped
¾ cup heavy whip cream
4-6 tablespoons parmesan cheese, grated

Directions:
Add leeks, chard, celery, 1 tablespoon garlic, oregano, salt, pepper and broth to your Ninja Foodi
Lock lid and cook on HIGH pressure for 3 minutes
Quick release pressure
Open lid and add more broth, set your pot to Sauté mode and adjust heat to HIGH
Add yellow squash, parsley and remaining 1 tablespoon garlic
Let it cook for 2-3 minutes until the squash is soft
Stir in cream and sprinkle parmesan
Serve

Nutrition Values (Per Serving):
Calories: 108
Fats: 8g
Carbs: 4g
Protein: 10g

Delicious Mushroom Stroganoff

Preparation Time: 10 minutes
Cooking Time: 15 minutes
Servings: 6
Ingredients:
¼ cup unsalted butter, cubed
1 pound cremini mushrooms, halved
1 large onion, halved
4 garlic cloves, minced
2 cups vegetable broth
½ teaspoon salt
¼ teaspoon fresh black pepper
1 and ½ cups sour cream
¼ cup fresh flat-leaf parsley, chopped
1 cup grated parmesan cheese
Directions:
Add butter, mushrooms, onion, garlic, vegetable broth, salt, pepper and paprika
Gently stir and lock lid
Cook on HIGH pressure for 5 minutes
Release pressure naturally over 10 minutes
Serve by stirring in sour cream and with a garnish of parsley and parmesan cheese.
Nutrition Values (Per Serving):
Calories: 218
Fats: 9g
Carbs: 4g
Protein: 10g

Everyday Use Veggie-Stock

Preparation Time: 2 hours
Cooking Time: 10 minutes
Servings: 6
Ingredients:
1 onion, quartered
2 large carrots, peeled and cut into 1 inch pieces
1 tablespoon olive oil
12 ounces mushrooms, sliced
¼ teaspoon salt
3 and ½ cups water

Directions:
Take cook and crisp basket out of the inner pot, close crisping lid and let it pre-heat for 3 minutes at 400 degrees F on Bake/Roast settings
While the pot heats up, add onion, carrot chunks in the Cook and Crisp basket and drizzle vegetable oil, toss well
Place basket back into the inner pot, close crisping lid and cook for 15 minutes at 400 degrees F on Bake/Roast mode
Make sure to shake the basket halfway through
Remove basket from pot and add onions, carrots, mushrooms, water and season with salt
Lock pressure lid and seal the valves, cook on HIGH pressure for 60 minutes
Release the pressure naturally over 10 minutes
Line a colander with cheesecloth and place it over a large bowl, pour vegetables and stock into the colander
Strain the stock and discard veggies

Nutrition Values (Per Serving):
Calories: 540
Fats: 2g
Carbs: 8g
Protein: 2g

Broccoli Florets

Preparation Time: 16 minutes
Cooking Time: 10 minutes
Servings: 4
Ingredients:
4 tablespoons butter, melted
Salt and pepper to taste
2 pounds broccoli florets
1 cup whipping cream
Directions:
Place a steamer basket in your Ninja Foodi (bottom part) and add water
Place florets on top of the basket and lock lid
Cook on HIGH pressure for 5 minutes
Quick release pressure
Transfer florets from the steamer basket to the pot
Add salt, pepper, butter and stir
Lock crisping lid and cook on Air Crisp mode for 360 degrees F
Serve
Nutrition Values (Per Serving):
Calories: 85
Fats: 0,3g
Carbs: 4,5g
Protein: 2,5g

Cauliflower And Cheddar Soup

Preparation Time: 5 minutes
Cooking Time: 16 minutes
Servings: 4
Ingredients:
¼ cup butter
½ sweet onion, chopped
1 head cauliflower, chopped
4 cups herbed vegetable stock
½ teaspoon ground nutmeg
1 cup heavy whip cream
Salt and pepper as needed
1 cup cheddar cheese, shredded
Directions:
Set your Ninja Foodi to sauté mode and add butter, let it heat up and melt
Add onion and Cauliflower, Sauté for 10 minutes until tender and lightly browned
Add vegetable stock and nutmeg, bring to a boil
Lock lid and cook on HIGH pressure for 5 minutes, quick release pressure once done
Remove pot and from Foodi and stir in heavy cream, puree using immersion blender
Season with more salt and pepper and serve with a topping of cheddar
Nutrition Values (Per Serving):
Calories: 228
Fats: 8g
Carbs: 2g
Protein: 2g

Butternut Squash Soup

Preparation Time: 5 minutes
Cooking Time: 10 minutes
Servings: 4
Ingredients:
1 ½ pounds butternut squash, baked, peeled and cubed
½ cup green onions, chopped
3 tablespoons butter
½ cup carrots, peeled and chopped
½ cup celery, chopped
29 ounces vegetable stock
1 garlic clove, peeled and minced
½ teaspoon Italian seasoning
15 ounces canned tomatoes, diced
Salt and pepper to taste
1/8 teaspoon red pepper flakes
1/8 teaspoon nutmeg, grated
1 and ½ cup half and half
Directions:
Set your Ninja Foodi to "Sauté" mode and add butter, let it melt
Add celery, carrots, onion and stir cook for 3 minutes
Add garlic, stir cook for 1 minute
Add squash, tomatoes, stock, Italian seasoning, salt, pepper, pepper flakes and nutmeg, stir
Lock lid and cook on HIGH pressure for 10 minutes
Release pressure naturally over 10 minutes
Use an immersion blender to puree the mix
Set the food to Sauté mode on LOW and add half and half, stir cook for 1-2 minutes until thickened
Divide and serve with a sprinkle of green onions on top
Nutrition Values (Per Serving):
Calories: 432
Fats: 4g
Carbs: 2g
Protein: 1g

Cauliflower Gratin

Preparation Time: 5 minutes
Cooking Time: 10 minutes
Servings: 4
Ingredients:
1 large cauliflower head, cup into florets
1 cup water
2 tsp salt
¼ tsp ground nutmeg
½ cup heavy cream
½ cup grated parmesan cheese
1 tbsp coconut flour
Directions
Add the water, salt, cauliflower and nutmeg to the bowl and place the lid on the machine, setting the steamer valve to seal. Use the pressure cooker function to cook the cauliflower on high pressure for 2 minutes. Do a quick pressure release and remove the lid once the timer is done.

Mix together the cream and coconut flour in a separate bowl. Add this mix to the pot and stir. Press the sauté button and bring the mix to a boil.

Sprinkle the cheese over the top and lower the air crisper lid. Set the temperature to 400 degrees and set the timer for 10 minutes. Cook until browned and then serve hot.
Nutrition Values (Per Serving):
Calories: 432
Fats: 5g
Carbs: 4g
Protein: 2g

Zucchini Fries

Preparation Time: 5 minutes
Cooking Time: 10 minutes
Servings: 4
Ingredients:
2 cups almond flour
2 Zucchinis
2 tsp salt
½ tsp ground black pepper
3 eggs
1 tbsp garlic powder
1 cup grated parmesan cheese
2 tsp onion powder
Directions
Cut the zucchini into strips about ¼ inch wide and 3 inches long. Sprinkle with the salt and let sit for about 20 minutes then pat dry to take any extra moisture off the fries
Add the almond flour and ground black pepper to a bowl and put the eggs in a separate small bowl and whisk briefly
In a third small bowl, mix the parmesan, garlic powder and onion powder together
Dip the fries one at a time in the flour then in the egg mix and finally in the cheese mix and set coated fries aside on a plate. Dip all the fries
Place the fries in the cook and crisp basket and then put the basket inside the pot. Lose the crisper lid and set the temperature to 375 degrees F and set the timer for 12 minutes
Serve fries while hot
Nutrition Values (Per Serving):
Calories: 121
Fats: 5g
Carbs: 2g
Protein: 2g

Fish and Seafood

Buttered Up Scallops

Preparation Time: 10 minutes
Cooking Time: 5 minutes
Servings: 4
Ingredients:
4 garlic cloves, minced
4 tablespoons rosemary, chopped
2 pounds sea scallops
12 cup butter
Salt and pepper to taste
Directions:
Set your Ninja Foodi to Saute mode and add butter, rosemary, and garlic
Saute for 1 minute. Add scallops, salt, and pepper
Saute for 2 minutes. Lock Crisping lid and Crisp for 3 minutes at 350 degrees F. Serve and enjoy!

Nutrition Values (Per Serving):

Calories: 279
Fat: 16g
Carbohydrates: 5g
Protein: 25g

Awesome Cherry Tomato Mackerel

Preparation Time: 5 minutes
Cooking Time: 7 minutes
Servings: 4

Ingredients:

4 Mackerel fillets
¼ teaspoon onion powder
¼ teaspoon lemon powder
¼ teaspoon garlic powder
½ teaspoon salt
2 cups cherry tomatoes
3 tablespoons melted butter
1 and ½ cups of water
1 tablespoon black olives

Directions:

Grease baking dish and arrange cherry tomatoes at the bottom of the dish
Top with fillets sprinkle all spices. Drizzle melted butter over
Add water to your Ninja Foodi
Lower rack in Ninja Foodi and place baking dish on top of the rack
Lock lid and cook on LOW pressure for 7 minutes. Quick release pressure. Serve and enjoy!

Nutrition Values (Per Serving):

Calories: 325
Fat: 24g
Carbohydrates: 2g
Protein: 21g

Lovely Air Fried Scallops

Preparation Time: 5 minutes
Cooking Time: 5 minutes
Servings: 4

Ingredients:

12 scallops
3 tablespoons olive oil
Salt and pepper to taste

Directions:

Gently rub scallops with salt, pepper, and oil
Transfer to your Ninja Foodie's insert, and place the insert in your Foodi
Lock Air Crisping lid and cook for 4 minutes at 390 degrees F
Half through, make sure to give them a nice flip and keep cooking. Serve warm and enjoy!

Nutrition Values (Per Serving):

Calories: 372
Fat: 11g
Carbohydrates: 0.9g
Protein: 63g

Packets Of Lemon And Dill Cod

Preparation Time: 10 minutes
Cooking Time: 10 minutes
Servings: 4
Ingredients:
2 tilapia cod fillets
Salt, pepper and garlic powder to taste
2 sprigs fresh dill
4 slices lemon
2 tablespoons butter
Directions:
Layout 2 large squares of parchment paper
Place fillet in center of each parchment square and season with salt, pepper and garlic powder
On each fillet, place 1 sprig of dill, 2 lemon slices, 1 tablespoon butter
Place trivet at the bottom of your Ninja Foodi. Add 1 cup water into the pot
Close parchment paper around fillets and fold to make a nice seal
Place both packets in your pot. Lock lid and cook on HIGH pressure for 5 minutes
Quick release pressure. Serve and enjoy!

Nutrition Values (Per Serving):

Calories: 259
Fat: 11g
Carbohydrates: 8g
Protein: 20g

Adventurous Sweet And Sour Fish

Preparation Time: 10 minutes
Cooking Time: 6 minutes
Servings: 2

Ingredients:

2 drops liquid stevia
¼ cup butter
1 pound fish chunks
1 tablespoon vinegar
Salt and pepper to taste

Directions:

Set your Ninja Foodi to Saute mode and add butter, let it melt
Add fish chunks and Saute for 3 minutes. Add stevia, salt, and pepper, stir
Lock Crisping Lid and cook on "Air Crisp" mode for 3 minutes at 360 degrees F
Serve once done and enjoy!

Nutrition Values (Per Serving):

Calories: 274
Fat: 15g
Carbohydrates: 2g
Protein: 33g

Cool Shrimp Zoodles

Preparation Time: 5 minutes
Cooking Time: 3 minutes
Servings: 4
Ingredients:
4 cups zoodles
1 tablespoon basil, chopped
2 tablespoons Ghee
1 cup vegetable stock
2 garlic cloves, minced
2 tablespoons olive oil
½ lemon
½ teaspoon paprika
Directions:
Set your Ninja Foodi to Saute mode and add ghee, let it heat up
Add olive oil as well. Add garlic and cook for 1 minute
Add lemon juice, shrimp and cook for 1 minute
Stir in rest of the ingredients and lock lid, cook on LOW pressure for 5 minutes
Quick release pressure and serve. Enjoy!
Nutrition Values (Per Serving):
Calories: 180
Fats: 3g
Carbs: 18g
Protein: 2g

Heartfelt Sesame Fish

Preparation Time: 8 minutes
Cooking Time: 8 minutes
Servings: 4
Ingredients:
1 and ½ pound salmon fillet
1 teaspoon sesame seeds
1 teaspoon butter, melted
½ teaspoon salt
1 tablespoon apple cider vinegar
¼ teaspoon rosemary, dried
Directions:
Take apple cider vinegar and spray it to the salmon fillets
Then add dried rosemary, sesame seeds, butter and salt
Mix them well. Take butter sauce and brush the salmon properly
Place the salmon on the rack and lower the air fryer lid. Set the air fryer mode
Cook the fish for 8 minutes at 360 F. Serve hot and enjoy!
Nutrition Values (Per Serving):
Calories: 234
Fats: 5g
Carbs: 9g
Protein: 12g

Awesome Sock-Eye Salmon

Preparation Time: 5 minutes
Cooking Time: 5 minutes
Servings: 4
Ingredients:
4 sockeye salmon fillets
1 teaspoon Dijon mustard
¼ teaspoon garlic, minced
¼ teaspoon onion powder
¼ teaspoon lemon pepper
½ teaspoon garlic powder
¼ teaspoon salt
2 tablespoons olive oil
1 and ½ cup of water
Directions:
Take a bowl and add mustard, lemon juice, onion powder, lemon pepper, garlic powder, salt, olive oil. Brush spice mix over salmon
Add water to Instant Pot. Place rack and place salmon fillets on rack
Lock lid and cook on LOW pressure for 7 minutes
Quick release pressure. Serve and enjoy!
Nutrition Values (Per Serving):
Calories: 432
Fats: 5g
Carbs: 4g
Protein: 2g

Buttered Up Scallops

Preparation Time: 10 minutes
Cooking Time: 5 minutes
Servings: 4
Ingredients:
4 garlic cloves, minced
4 tablespoons rosemary, chopped
2 pounds sea scallops
12 cup butter
Salt and pepper to taste

Directions:
Set your Ninja Foodi to Saute mode and add butter, rosemary, and garlic
Saute for 1 minute. Add scallops, salt, and pepper
Saute for 2 minutes. Lock Crisping lid and Crisp for 3 minutes at 350 degrees F. Serve and enjoy!

Nutrition Values (Per Serving):
Calories: 128
Fats: 3g
Carbs: 3g
Protein: 5g

Cherry Tomato Mackerel

Preparation Time: 5 minutes
Cooking Time: 7 minutes
Servings: 4
Ingredients:
4 Mackerel fillets
¼ teaspoon onion powder
¼ teaspoon lemon powder
¼ teaspoon garlic powder
½ teaspoon salt
2 cups cherry tomatoes
3 tablespoons melted butter
1 and ½ cups of water
1 tablespoon black olives

Directions:
Grease baking dish and arrange cherry tomatoes at the bottom of the dish
Top with fillets sprinkle all spices. Drizzle melted butter over
Add water to your Ninja Foodi
Lower rack in Ninja Foodi and place baking dish on top of the rack
Lock lid and cook on LOW pressure for 7 minutes. Quick release pressure. Serve and enjoy!

Nutrition Values (Per Serving):
Calories: 297
Fats: 3g
Carbs: 8g
Protein: 5g

Garlic And Lemon Prawn Delight

Preparation Time: 5 minutes
Cooking Time: 5 minutes
Servings: 4

Ingredients:

2 tablespoons olive oil
1 pound prawns
2 tablespoons garlic, minced
2/3 cup fish stock
1 tablespoon butter
2 tablespoons lemon juice
1 tablespoon lemon zest
Salt and pepper to taste

Directions:

Set your Ninja Foodi to Saute mode and add butter and oil, let it heat up
Stir in remaining ingredients. Lock lid and cook on LOW pressure for 5 minutes
Quick release pressure. Serve and enjoy!

Nutrition Values (Per Serving):

Calories: 236
Fat: 12g
Carbohydrates: 2g
Protein: 27g

Lovely Carb Soup

Preparation Time: 5 minutes
Cooking Time: 6 hours 0 minutes
Servings: 2
Ingredients:
Ingredients
1 cup crab meat, cubed
1 tablespoon garlic, minced
Salt as needed
Red chili flakes as needed
3 cups vegetable broth
1 teaspoon salt

Directions:
Coat the crab cubes in lime juice and let them sit for a while
Add the all ingredients (including marinated crab meat):to your Ninja Foodi and lock lid
Cook on SLOW COOK MODE (MEDIUM) for 3 hours
Let it sit for a while
Unlock lid and set to Saute mode, simmer the soup for 5 minutes more on LOW
Stir and check to season. Enjoy!

Nutrition Values (Per Serving):

Calories: 201
Fat: 11g
Carbohydrates: 12g
Protein: 13g

The Rich Guy Lobster And Butter

Preparation Time: 15 minutes
Cooking Time: 20 minutes
Servings: 4
Ingredients
6 Lobster Tails
4 garlic cloves,
¼ cup butter
Directions:
Preheat the Ninja Foodi to 400 degrees F at first
Open the lobster tails gently by using kitchen scissors
Remove the lobster meat gently from the shells but keep it inside the shells
Take a plate and place it
Add some butter in a pan and allow it melt
Put some garlic cloves in it and heat it over medium-low heat
Pour the garlic butter mixture all over the lobster tail meat
Let the fryer to broil the lobster at 130 degrees F
Remove the lobster meat from Ninja Foodi and set aside
Use a fork to pull out the lobster meat from the shells entirely
Pour some garlic butter over it if needed. Serve and enjoy!

Nutrition Values (Per Serving):

Calories: 160
Fat: 1g
Carbohydrates: 1g
Protein: 20g

Lovely Panko Cod

Preparation Time: 5 minutes
Cooking Time: 15 minutes
Servings: 6

Ingredients:

2 uncooked cod fillets, 6 ounces each
3 teaspoons kosher salt
¾ cup panko bread crumbs
2 tablespoons butter, melted
¼ cup fresh parsley, minced
1 lemon. Zested and juiced

Directions:

Pre-heat your Ninja Foodi at 390 degrees F and place Air Crisper basket inside
Season cod and salt
Take a bowl and add bread crumbs, parsley, lemon juice, zest, butter, and mix well
Coat fillets with the bread crumbs mixture and place fillets in your Air Crisping basket
Lock Air Crisping lid and cook on Air Crisp mode for 15 minutes at 360 degrees F
Serve and enjoy!

Nutrition Values (Per Serving):

Calories: 554
Fat: 24g
Carbohydrates: 5g
Protein: 37g

Salmon Paprika

Preparation Time: 5 minutes
Cooking Time: 7 minutes
Servings: 4

Ingredients:

2 wild caught salmon fillets, 1 to 1 and ½ inches thick
2 teaspoons avocado oil
2 teaspoons paprika
Salt and pepper to taste
Green herbs to garnish

Directions:

Season salmon fillets with salt, pepper, paprika, and olive oil
Place Crisping basket in your Ninja Foodi, and pre-heat your Ninja Foodie at 390 degrees F
Place insert insider your Foodi and place the fillet in the insert, lock Air Crisping lid and cook for 7 minutes. Once done, serve the fish with herbs on top. Enjoy!

Nutrition Values (Per Serving):

Calories: 249
Fat: 11g
Carbohydrates: 1.8g
Protein: 35g

Heartfelt Air Fried Scampi

Preparation Time: 5 minutes
Cooking Time: 5 minutes
Servings: 4

Ingredients:

4 tablespoons butter
1 tablespoon lemon juice
1 tablespoon garlic, minced
2 teaspoons red pepper flakes
1 tablespoon chives, chopped
1 tablespoon basil leaves, minced
2 tablespoons chicken stock
1 pound defrosted shrimp

Directions:

Set your Foodi to Saute mode and add butter, let the butter melt and add red pepper flakes and garlic, Saute for 2 minutes

Transfer garlic to crisping basket, add remaining ingredients (including shrimp) to the basket

Return basket back to the Ninja Foodi and lock the Air Crisping lid, cook for 5 minutes at 390 degrees F. Once done, serve with a garnish of fresh basil

Nutrition Values (Per Serving):

Calories: 372
Fat: 11g
Carbohydrates: 0.9g
Protein: 63g

Ranch Warm Fillets

Preparation Time: 5 minutes
Cooking Time: 13 minutes
Servings: 4

Ingredients:

¼ cup panko
½ packet ranch dressing mix powder
1 and ¼ tablespoons vegetable oil
1 egg beaten
2 tilapia fillets
A garnish of herbs and chilies

Directions:

Pre-heat your Ninja Foodi with the Crisping Basket inside at 350 degrees F
Take a bowl and mix in ranch dressing and panko
Beat eggs in a shallow bowl and keep it on the side
Dip fillets in the eggs, then in the panko mix
Place fillets in your Ninja Foodie's insert and transfer insert to Ninja Foodi
Lock Air Crisping Lid and Air Crisp for 13 minutes at 350 degrees F
Garnish with chilies and herbs. Enjoy!

Nutrition Values (Per Serving):

Calories: 301
Fat: 12g
Carbohydrates: 1.5g
Protein: 28g

Orange Sauce And Salmon

Preparation Time: 30 minutes
Cooking Time: 15 minutes
Servings: 4

Ingredients:

1 pound salmon
1 tablespoon coconut amino
2 teaspoons ginger, minced
1 teaspoon garlic, minced
1 teaspoon salt
2 tablespoons sugar marmalade

Directions:

Take a zip bag and add the Salmon. Take a bowl and add all of the ingredients and mix well

Pour the mixture into the salmon container bag and mix well to ensure that the salmon is coated well. Allow it to marinate for 30 minutes

Add 2 cups of water to the Ninja Foodi. Carefully put a steamer rack/trivet on top of your Foodi

Add the marinated salmon and sauce on the rack

Lock up the lid and cook on LOW pressure for 3 minutes

Allow the pressure to release naturally. Serve or broil for 3-4 minutes for a brown texture

Alternatively, you may bake the salmon at 350 degrees Fahrenheit for a slightly flaky fish. Enjoy!

Nutrition Values (Per Serving):

Calories: 166
Fats: 7g
Carbs:8g
Protein:25g

Cucumber And Salmon Mix

Preparation Time: 5 minutes
Cooking Time: 5 minutes
Servings: 4
Ingredients:
1 pound salmon steaks
½ cup plain low-fat Greek yogurt
½ cup cucumber, peeled and diced
1 tablespoon fresh dill, chopped
1 tablespoon olive oil
½ teaspoon ground coriander
1 teaspoon fresh lemon juice
1 cup of water
Salt and pepper to taste
Directions:
Mix in low-fat Greek yogurt, dill, cucumber, a pinch of salt and pepper each, mix well and put in the fridge
Brush salmon steaks with olive oil, season salmon with salt, pepper and coriander and lemon juice. Add water to Ninja Foodi and place a steamer rack
Add fish fillets on rack and lock lid. Cook on HIGH pressure for 3 minutes
Release pressure naturally over 10 minutes. Open the lid and serve salmon with cucumber sauce. Enjoy!

Nutrition Values (Per Serving):

Calories: 406
Fat: 5g
Carbohydrates: 4g
Protein: 50g

Poultry and Meat

Mexican Beef Dish

Preparation Time: 5 minutes
Cooking Time: 12 minutes
Servings: 4

Ingredients:

2 and ½ pounds boneless beef short ribs
1 tablespoon chili powder
1 and ½ teaspoons salt
1 tablespoon fat
1 medium onion, thinly sliced
1 tablespoon tomato sauce
6 garlic cloves, peeled and smashed
½ cup roasted tomato salsa
½ cup bone broth
Fresh ground black pepper
½ cup cilantro, minced
2 radishes, sliced

Directions:

Take a large sized bowl and add the cubed beef, salt, and chili powder, give it a nice mix
Set your Ninja Foodi to Saute mode and add butter, allow it to melt
Add garlic and tomato paste and Saute for 30 seconds. Add seasoned beef, stock and fish sauce
Lock up the lid and cook on HIGH pressure for 35 minutes on MEAT/STEW mode
Release the pressure naturally over 10 minutes. Season with some salt and pepper and enjoy!

Nutrition Values (Per Serving):

Calories: 308
Fats: 18g
Carbs:21g
Protein:38g

All-Tim Favorite Beef Chili

Preparation Time: 10 minutes
Cooking Time: 40 minutes
Servings: 4

Ingredients:

1 and ½ pounds ground beef
1 sweet onion, peeled and chopped
Salt and pepper to taste
28 ounces canned tomatoes, diced
17 ounces beef stock
6 garlic cloves, peeled and chopped
7 jalapeno peppers, diced
2 tablespoons olive oil
4 carrots, peeled and chopped
3 tablespoons chili powder
1 bay leaf
1 teaspoon chili powder

Directions:

Set your Ninja Foodi to "Saute" mode and add half of the oil, let it heat up
Add beef and stir brown for 8 minutes, transfer to a bowl
Add remaining oil to the pot and let it heat up, add carrots, onion, jalapenos, garlic and stir Saute for 4 minutes. Add tomatoes and stir
Add bay leaf, stock, chili powder, chili powder, salt, pepper, and beef, stir and lock lid
Cook on HIGH pressure for 25 minutes. Release pressure naturally over 10 minutes
Stir the chili and serve. Enjoy!

Nutrition Values (Per Serving):

Calories: 448
Fat: 22g
Carbohydrates: 7g
Protein: 15g

Ingenious Bo Kho

Preparation Time: 5 minutes
Cooking Time: 45 minutes
Servings: 6
Ingredients:
½ teaspoon ghee
2 and ½ pounds grass-fed beef brisket
1 yellow onion, peeled and diced
1 and ½ teaspoon curry powder
2 and ½ tablespoons fresh ginger, peeled
2 cups tomatoes, drained and crushed
3 tablespoons red boat fish sauce
1 large stalk lemongrass
2 whole star anise
1 bay leaf
1 cup bone broth

Directions:
Set your Ninja Foodi to Saute mode and add ghee
Allow it to melt. Add briskets. Keep frying them until they have a nice brown texture
Remove the brisket and add onion and Saute them
Add curry powder, ginger, seared beef, fish sauce, star anise, diced tomatoes
Stir well and add bay leaf and lemongrass. Pour broth and lock up the lid
Cook for 35 minutes at HIGH pressure. Allow the pressure to release naturally
Add carrots. Cook for another 7 minutes at HIGH pressure
Release the pressure naturally. Serve hot!

Nutrition Values (Per Serving):

Calories: 462
Fats: 20g
Carbs:15g
Protein:54g

Sesame Beef Ribs

Preparation Time: 10 minutes
Cooking Time: 60 minutes
Servings: 6

Ingredients:

1 tablespoon sesame oil
2 garlic cloves, peeled and smashed
Knob fresh ginger, peeled and finely chopped
1 pinch red pepper flakes
¼ cup white wine vinegar
2/3 cup coconut aminos
2/3 cup beef stock
4 pounds beef ribs, chopped in half
2 tablespoons arrowroot
1-2 tablespoons water

Directions:

Set your Ninja Foodi to Saute mode and add sesame oil, garlic, ginger, red pepper flakes and Saute for 1 minute. Deglaze pot with vinegar and mix in coconut aminos and beef stock
Add ribs to the pot and coat them well. Lock lid and cook on HIGH pressure for 60 minutes
Release pressure naturally over 10 minutes. Remove the ribs and keep them on the side
Take a small bowl and mix in arrowroot and water, stir and mix in the liquid into the pot, set the pot to Saute mode and cook until the liquid reaches your desired consistency
Put the ribs under a broiler to brown them slightly (also possible to do this in the Ninja Foodi using the Air Crisping lid). Serve ribs with the cooking liquid. Enjoy!

Nutrition Values (Per Serving):

Calories: 307
Fat: 10g
Carbohydrates: 5g
Protein: 32g

The Chipotle Copycat Dish

Preparation Time: 5 minutes
Cooking Time: 90 minutes
Servings: 6
Ingredients:
3 pounds grass-fed chuck roast, large chunks
1 large onion, peeled and sliced
6 garlic cloves
2 cans (14.5 ounces):green chilies
1 tablespoon oregano
1 teaspoon salt and pepper
3 dried chipotle pepper, stems removed, broken into small pieces
Juice of 3 limes
3 tablespoons coconut vinegar
1 tablespoon cumin
½ cup of water

Directions:
Add the listed ingredients to your Ninja Foodi
Stir and lock up the lid, cook on HIGH pressure for 60 minutes
Release the pressure naturally over 10 minutes. Remove the lid and shred using a fork
Set your pot to Saute mode and reduce for 30 minutes. Enjoy once ready!

Nutrition Values (Per Serving):

Calories: 831
Fat: 62g
Carbohydrates: 5g
Protein: 61g

All-Buttered Up Beef

Preparation Time: 5 minutes
Cooking Time: 60 minutes
Servings: 6
Ingredients:
3 pounds beef roast
1 tablespoon olive oil
2 tablespoons Keto-Friendly ranch dressing
1 jar pepper rings, with juices
8 tablespoons butter
1 cup of water

Directions:
Set your Ninja Foodi to Saute mode and add 1 tablespoon of oil
Once the oil is hot, add roast and sear both sides
Set the Saute off and add water, seasoning mix, reserved juice, and pepper rings on top of your beef. Lock up the lid and cook on HIGH pressure for 60 minutes
Release the pressure naturally over 10 minutes. Cut the beef with salad sheers and serve with pureed cauliflower. Enjoy!

Nutrition Values (Per Serving):

Calories: 269
Fat: 18g
Carbohydrates: 12g
Protein: 16g

Bruschetta Chicken Meal

Preparation Time: 5 minutes
Cooking Time: 9 minutes
Servings: 4
Ingredients:
2 tablespoons balsamic vinegar
1/3 cup olive oil
2 teaspoons garlic cloves, minced
1 teaspoon black pepper
½ teaspoon salt
½ cup sun-dried tomatoes, in olive oil
2 pounds chicken breasts, quartered, boneless
2 tablespoons fresh basil, chopped
Direction:
Take a bowl and whisk in vinegar, oil, garlic, pepper, salt
Fold in tomatoes, basil and add breast, mix well. Transfer to fridge and let it sit for 30 minutes
Add everything to Ninja Foodi and lock lid, cook on High Pressure for 9 minutes
Quick release pressure. Serve and enjoy!
Nutrition Values (Per Serving):
Calories: 221
Fats: 3g
Carbs: 2g
Protein: 5g

The Great Hainanese Chicken

Preparation Time: 20 minutes
Cooking Time: 4 hours 0 minutes
Servings: 4
Ingredients:
1 ounces ginger, peeled
6 garlic cloves, crushed
6 bundles cilantro/basil leaves
1 teaspoon salt
1 tablespoon sesame oil
3 (1 and ½ pounds each) chicken meat, ready to cook
For Dip
2 tablespoons ginger, minced
1 teaspoon garlic, minced
1 tablespoon chicken stock
1 teaspoon sesame oil
½ teaspoon sugar
Salt to taste
Directions:
Add chicken, garlic, ginger, leaves, and salt in your Ninja Food
Add enough water to fully submerge chicken, lock lid cook on SLOW COOK mode on LOW for 4 hours. Release pressure naturally
Take chicken out of pot and chill for 10 minutes
Take a bowl and add all the dipping ingredients and blend well in a food processor
Take chicken out of ice bath and drain, chop into serving pieces. Arrange onto a serving platter
Brush chicken with sesame oil. Serve with ginger dip. Enjoy!
Nutrition Values (Per Serving):
Calories: 123
Fats: 5g
Carbs: 6g
Protein: 2g

A Genuine Hassel Back Chicken

Preparation Time: 5 minutes
Cooking Time: 60 minutes
Servings: 4
Ingredients:
4 tablespoons butter
Salt and pepper to taste
2 cups fresh mozzarella cheese, thinly sliced
8 large chicken breasts
4 large Roma tomatoes, thinly sliced

Directions:
Make few deep slits in chicken breasts, season with salt and pepper
Stuff mozzarella cheese slices and tomatoes in chicken slits
Grease Ninja Foodi pot with butter and arrange stuffed chicken breasts
Lock lid and BAKE/ROAST for 1 hour at 365 degrees F. Serve and enjoy!
Nutrition Values (Per Serving):
Calories: 287
Fats: 8g
Carbs: 4g
Protein: 5g

Shredded Up Salsa Chicken

Preparation Time: 5 minutes
Cooking Time: 20 minutes
Servings: 4
Ingredients:
1 pound chicken breast, skin and bones removed
¾ teaspoon cumin
½ teaspoon salt
Pinch of oregano
Pepper to taste
1 cup chunky salsa Keto friendly
Directions:
Season chicken with spices and add to Ninja Foodi
Cover with salsa and lock lid, cook on HIGH pressure for 20 minutes
Quick release pressure. Add chicken to a platter and shred the chicken. Serve and enjoy!
Nutrition Values (Per Serving):
Calories: 321
Fats: 2g
Carbs: 8g
Protein: 5g

Mexico's Favorite Chicken Soup

Preparation Time: 5 minutes
Cooking Time: 20 minutes
Servings: 4
Ingredients:
2 cups chicken, shredded
4 tablespoons olive oil
½ cup cilantro, chopped
8 cups chicken broth
1/3 cup salsa
1 teaspoon onion powder
½ cup scallions, chopped
4 ounces green chilies, chopped
½ teaspoon habanero, minced
1 cup celery root, chopped
1 teaspoon cumin
1 teaspoon garlic powder
Salt and pepper to taste

Directions:
Add all ingredients to Ninja Foodi. Stir and lock lid, cook on HIGH pressure for 10 minutes
Release pressure naturally over 10 minutes. Serve and enjoy!

Nutrition Values (Per Serving):
Calories: 187
Fats: 18g
Carbs: 3g
Protein: 22g

Taiwanese Chicken Delight

Preparation Time: 5 minutes
Cooking Time: 10 minutes
Servings: 4
Ingredients:
6 dried red chilis
¼ cup sesame oil
2 tablespoons ginger
¼ cup garlic, minced
¼ cup red wine vinegar
¼ cup coconut aminos
Salt as needed
1.2 teaspoon xanthan gum (for the finish):
¼ cup Thai basil, chopped
Directions:
Set your Ninja Foodi to Saute mode and add ginger, chilis, garlic and Saute for 2 minutes
Add remaining ingredients. Lock lid and cook on HIGH pressure for 10 minutes
Quick release pressure. Serve and enjoy!
Nutrition Values (Per Serving):
Calories: 212
Fats: 8g
Carbs: 4g
Protein: 28g

Beef And Broccoli Delight

Preparation Time: 5 minutes
Cooking Time: 6 hours 0 minutes
Servings: 6
Ingredients:
1 and ½ pounds beef round steak, cut into 2 inches by 1/8 inch strips
1 cup broccoli, diced
½ teaspoon red pepper flakes
2 teaspoon garlic, minced
2 teaspoons olive oil
2 tablespoons apple cider vinegar
2 tablespoons coconut aminos
2 tablespoons white wine vinegar
1 tablespoons arrowroot
¼ cup beef broth

Directions:
Take a large sized bowl and make the sauce by mixing in red pepper flakes, olive oil, coconut aminos, garlic, white wine vinegar, apple cider vinegar, broth and arrowroot
Mix well. Add the mix to your Ninja Foodi. Add beef and place a lid
Cook on SLOW COOK MODE (LOW) for 6-8 hours
Uncover just 30 minutes before end time and add broccoli, lock lid again and let it finish
Serve and enjoy!

Nutrition Values (Per Serving):

Calories: 208
Fat: 12g
Carbohydrates: 11g
Protein: 15g

Rich Beef Rendang

Preparation Time: 5 minutes
Cooking Time: 25 minutes
Servings: 6
Ingredients:
1 cup onion, chopped
1 tablespoon ginger, chopped
1 tablespoon garlic, minced
1 small jalapeno pepper
2 tablespoons olive oil
1 pack rendang curry paste
1 pound skirt steak, cut into 2 inch chunks
½ cup of water
1 cup coconut milk (full fat):
2 tablespoons coconut, shredded

Directions:
Mince the onion, garlic, and ginger. Set your Ninja Foodi to Saute mode and add oil Allow the oil to heat up and add veggies and stir them well. Add rending paste and stir for 3-4 minutes. Add skirt steak and stir to coat with the spices for about 2 minutes Pour ¼ cup of water and deglazed. Lock up the lid and cook on HIGH pressure for 25 minutes
Release the pressure naturally over 10 minutes. Add ½ a cup of coconut milk and stir Garnish with shredded coconut and serve!

Nutrition Values (Per Serving):

Calories: 271
Fat: 20g
Carbohydrates: 5g
Protein: 13g

Spiritual Indian Beef Dish

Preparation Time: 15 minutes
Cooking Time: 20 minutes
Servings: 4
Ingredients:
½ yellow onion, chopped
1 tablespoon olive oil
2 garlic cloves, minced
1 jalapeno pepper, chopped
1 cup cherry tomatoes, quartered
1 teaspoon fresh lemon juice
1-2 pounds grass-fed ground beef
1-2 pounds fresh collard greens, trimmed and chopped
Spices
1 teaspoon cumin, ground
½ teaspoon ginger, ground
1 teaspoon coriander, ground
½ teaspoon fennel seeds, ground
½ teaspoon cinnamon, ground
Salt and pepper to taste
½ teaspoon turmeric, ground

Directions:
Set your Ninja Foodi to sauté mode and add garlic, onions
sauté for 3 minutes. Add jalapeno pepper, beef, and spices
Lock lid and cook on Medium-HIGH pressure for 15 minutes
Release pressure naturally over 10 minutes, open lid
Add tomatoes, collard greens and sauté for 3 minutes
Stir in lemon juice, salt, and pepper. Stir well
Once the dish is ready, transfer the dish to your serving bowl and enjoy!

Nutrition Values (Per Serving):

Calories: 409
Fat: 16g
Carbohydrates: 5g
Protein: 56g

Shredded Up Salsa Chicken

Preparation Time: 5 minutes
Cooking Time: 20 minutes
Servings: 4
Ingredients:
1 pound chicken breast, skin and bones removed
¾ teaspoon cumin
½ teaspoon salt
Pinch of oregano
Pepper to taste
1 cup chunky salsa Keto friendly
Directions:
Season chicken with spices and add to Ninja Foodi
Cover with salsa and lock lid, cook on HIGH pressure for 20 minutes
Quick release pressure. Add chicken to a platter and shred the chicken. Serve and enjoy!

Nutrition Values (Per Serving):

Calories: 125
Fat: 3g
Carbohydrates: 2g
Protein: 22g

Mexico's Favorite Chicken Soup

Preparation Time: 5 minutes
Cooking Time: 20 minutes
Servings: 4
Ingredients:
2 cups chicken, shredded
4 tablespoons olive oil
½ cup cilantro, chopped
8 cups chicken broth
1/3 cup salsa
1 teaspoon onion powder
½ cup scallions, chopped
4 ounces green chilies, chopped
½ teaspoon habanero, minced
1 cup celery root, chopped
1 teaspoon cumin
1 teaspoon garlic powder
Salt and pepper to taste

Directions:
Add all ingredients to Ninja Foodi. Stir and lock lid, cook on HIGH pressure for 10 minutes
Release pressure naturally over 10 minutes. Serve and enjoy!

Nutrition Values (Per Serving):

Calories: 204
Fat: 14g
Carbohydrates: 4g
Protein: 14g

Taiwanese Chicken Delight

Preparation Time: 5 minutes
Cooking Time: 10 minutes
Servings: 4
Ingredients:
6 dried red chilis
¼ cup sesame oil
2 tablespoons ginger
¼ cup garlic, minced
¼ cup red wine vinegar
¼ cup coconut aminos
Salt as needed
1.2 teaspoon xanthan gum (for the finish):
¼ cup Thai basil, chopped
Directions:
Set your Ninja Foodi to Saute mode and add ginger, chilis, garlic and Saute for 2 minutes
Add remaining ingredients. Lock lid and cook on HIGH pressure for 10 minutes
Quick release pressure. Serve and enjoy!

Nutrition Values (Per Serving):

Calories: 307
Fat: 15g
Carbohydrates: 7g
Protein: 31g

Cabbage And Chicken Meatballs

Preparation Time: 10 minutes
Cooking Time: 30 minutes
Servings: 4
Ingredients:
1 pound ground chicken
¼ cup heavy whip cream
2 teaspoons salt
½ teaspoon ground caraway seeds
1 and ½ teaspoons fresh ground black pepper, divided
1/4 teaspoon ground allspice
4-6 cups green cabbage, thickly chopped
½ cup almond milk
2 tablespoons unsalted butter

Directions:
Transfer meat to a bowl and add cream, 1 teaspoon salt, caraway, ½ teaspoon pepper, allspice and mix it well. Let the mixture chill for 30 minutes
Once the mixture is ready, use your hands to scoop the mixture into meatballs
Add half of your balls to Ninja Foodi pot and cover with half of the cabbage
Add remaining balls and cover with rest of the cabbage
Add milk, pats of butter, season with salt and pepper
Lock lid and cook on HIGH pressure for 4 minutes. Quick release pressure
Unlock lid and serve. Enjoy!

Nutrition Values (Per Serving):

Calories: 294
Fat: 26g
Carbohydrates: 4g
Protein: 12g

Poached Chicken With Coconut Lime Cream Sauce

Preparation Time: 5 minutes
Cooking Time: 10 minutes
Servings: 4
Ingredients:
1-ounce shallot, minced
1 ounces ginger, sliced
2 medium banana peppers,
1 cup of coconut milk
1 cup chicken stock
Juice of 1 lime, and zest
2 tablespoons fish sauce
3 pieces of 1/3 pounds each chicken breasts, meat
Directions:
Add listed ingredients to your Ninja Foodi
Stir well and lock lid, cook on HIGH pressure for 10 minutes
Quick release pressure. Top with fresh cilantro. Serve and enjoy!

Nutrition Values (Per Serving):

Calories: 425
Fat: 33g
Carbohydrates: 9g
Protein: 24g

Hot And Spicy Paprika Chicken

Preparation Time: 10 minutes
Cooking Time: 20 minutes
Servings: 4
Ingredients:
4 piece (4 ounces each):chicken breast, skin on
Salt and pepper to taste
½ cup sweet onion, chopped
½ cup heavy whip cream
2 teaspoons smoked paprika
½ cup sour cream
2 tablespoons fresh parsley, chopped
Directions:
Season chicken with salt and pepper
Set your Foodi to Saute mode and add oil, let it heat up
Add chicken and sear both sides until nicely browned. Should take around 15 minutes
Remove chicken and transfer to a plate
Take a skillet and place it over medium heat, add onion and Sauté for 4 minutes
Stir in cream, paprika, bring the liquid to simmer. Return chicken to skillet and warm
Transfer the whole mixture to your Foodi and lock lid, cook on HIGH pressure for 5 minutes
Release pressure naturally over 10 minutes. Stir in cream, serve and enjoy!

Nutrition Values (Per Serving):

Calories: 389
Fat: 30g
Carbohydrates: 4g
Protein: 25g

Beef Lamb and Pork

Fried Meatballs with Tomato Sauce

Preparation Time: 5 minutes
Cooking Time: 35 minutes
Servings: 2
Ingredients:
1 small onion
1 pound minced beef
1 tbsp. chopped parsley
1 tbsp. chopped thyme leaves
1 egg, beaten
3 tbsp. bread crumbs
3/4 cup of your favorite tomato sauce.
Salt and pepper, to taste
Directions:
Place in the ceramic pot the Ninja Foodi Cook and Crisp basket.
In a mixing bowl, combine all ingredients except for the tomato sauce.
Form small balls using your hands.
Place the balls in the basket.
Close the crisping lid and press the Air Crisp button before pressing the START button.
Adjust the cooking time to 20 minutes.
Give the basket a shape halfway through the cooking time to evenly cook the food.
Once cooked, pour over your favorite tomato sauce on top. Serve and enjoy!
Nutrition Values (Per Serving):
Calories: 324
Fats: 6g
Carbs: 9g
Protein: 15g

Keto Baked Beef Brisket

Preparation Time: 5 minutes
Cooking Time: 50 minutes
Servings: 14
Ingredients:
20 garlic cloves, minced
2 bunches cilantro, chopped
1 1/4 cups red wine vinegar
3 onions, sliced thinly
8 pounds beef brisket
Direction:
Place in the ceramic pot the Foodi Cook and Crisp reversible rack.
In a blender, place the garlic, cilantro, red wine, and onions. Pulse until smooth.
Place the mixture in a Ziploc bag and add in the beef brisket.
Season with salt and pepper to taste.
Allow to marinate in the fridge for at least 2 hours.
Place the marinated brisket on the rack.
Close the crisping lid and press the Bake/Roast button before pressing the START button.
Adjust the cooking time to 60 minutes.
Meanwhile, place the marinade in a saucepan and bring to a simmer until the sauce is reduced.
Use the sauce to brush on the beef brisket halfway through the cooking time. Serve and enjoy!
Nutrition Values (Per Serving):
Calories: 180
Fats: 3g
Carbs: 4g
Protein: 12g

Pork Chops in Honey Mustard Sauce

Preparation Time: 5 minutes
Cooking Time: 10 minutes
Servings: 4
Ingredients:
2 tbsp. honey
4 tbsp. mustard
2 tbsp. garlic, minced
Salt and pepper, to taste
4 pork chops
Cooking spray
Directions:
Mix the honey, mustard, garlic, salt and pepper in a bowl.
Marinate the pork chops in the mixture for 20 minutes.
Place the pork chops on the Ninja Foodi basket.
Put the basket inside the pot.
Seal with the crisping lid.
Set it to air crisp.
Cook at 350 degrees F for 12 minutes, flipping halfway through.
Serve with rice or noodles. Enjoy!
Nutrition Values (Per Serving):
Calories: 143
Fats: 7g
Carbs: 2g
Protein: 18g

Air Fried Pork Chops

Preparation Time: 5 minutes
Cooking Time: 10 minutes
Servings: 2
Ingredients:
6 pork chops
Salt and pepper, to taste
1/2 cup bread crumbs
2 tbsp. Parmesan cheese, grated
1/4 cup cornflakes, crushed
1 1/4 tsp. sweet paprika
1/2 tsp. onion powder
1/2 tsp. garlic powder
1 egg, beaten
Directions:
Season the pork chops with salt and pepper.
In a bowl, mix the rest of the ingredients except the egg.
Beat the egg in a bowl.
Dip the pork chops in the egg.
Coat the pork with the breading.
Place the pork on the Ninja Foodi basket.
Set it to air crisp and close the crisping lid.
Cook at 400 degrees F for 12 minutes, flipping halfway through.
You can serve with mashed potatoes and gravy. Enjoy!
Nutrition Values (Per Serving):
Calories: 350
Fats: 3g
Carbs: 2g
Protein: 29g

Keto Garlic Butter Pork

Preparation Time: 20 minutes
Cooking Time: 1 hour 20 minutes
Servings: 2
Ingredients:
1 tbsp. coconut butter
1 tbsp. coconut oil
2 tsp. garlic cloves, grated
2 tsp. parsley
Salt and pepper, to taste
4 pork chops, sliced into strips
Directions:
Combine all the ingredients except the pork strips and then mix well.
Marinate the pork in the mixture for 1 hour.
Put the pork on the Ninja Foodi basket.
Set it inside the pot.
Seal with the crisping lid.
Choose air crisp function.
Cook at 400 degrees for 10 minutes.
Serve with fresh garden salad. Enjoy!
Nutrition Values (Per Serving):
Calories: 340
Fats: 4g
Carbs: 8g
Protein: 13g

Mediterranean Lamb Roast

Preparation Time: 10 minutes
Cooking Time: 1 hour 40 minutes
Servings: 4
Ingredients:
2 tbsp. olive oil
5 lb. leg of lamb
Salt and pepper, to taste
1 tsp. dried marjoram
3 garlic cloves, minced
1 tsp. dried sage
1 tsp. dried thyme
1 tsp. ground ginger
1 bay leaf, crushed
2 cups broth
3 lb. potatoes, sliced into cubes
2 tbsp. arrowroot powder
1/3 cup water
Directions:
Set the Ninja Foodi to Sauté.
Pour in the olive oil and then add the lamb.
Coat with the oil.
Season with the herbs and spices.
Sear on both sides.
Pour in the broth.
Add the potatoes.
Close the pot and then set it to pressure.
Cook at high pressure for 50 minutes.
Release the pressure naturally.
Dissolve the arrowroot powder in water.
Stir in the diluted arrowroot powder into the cooking liquid.
Let it sit for a few minutes before serving.
You can serve with cauliflower rice. Enjoy!
Nutrition Values (Per Serving):
Calories: 298
Fats: 3g
Carbs: 7g
Protein: 32g

Rosemary Lamb Chops

Preparation Time: 10 minutes
Cooking Time: 20 minutes
Servings: 6
Ingredients:
3 lb. lamb chops
4 rosemary sprigs
Salt, to taste
1 tbsp. olive oil
2 tbsp. butter
1 tbsp. tomato paste
1 cup beef stock
1 green onion, sliced
Directions:
Season the lamb chops with rosemary, salt and pepper.
Pour in the olive oil and add the butter to the Ninja Foodi and set it to sauté.
Add the lamb chops and cook for one minute per side.
Add the rest of the ingredients and stir well.
Cover the pot and set it to pressure.
Cook at high pressure for 5 minutes.
Release pressure naturally.
You can serve with pickled onions. Enjoy!
Nutrition Values (Per Serving):
Calories: 213
Fats: 6g
Carbs: 2g
Protein: 24g

Pork Carnitas

Preparation Time: 10 minutes
Cooking Time: 40 minutes
Servings: 4
Ingredients:
2 pounds pork butt, chopped into large cubes
1 tsp. salt
1/2 tsp. oregano
1/2 tsp. cumin
1 orange, cut in half and juiced
6 garlic cloves, peeled and crushed
1 cup chicken broth
Directions:
Place the ceramic pot in the Ninja Foodi base and the put all the ingredients in it.
Put the pressure lid and make sure that the vent is on the SEAL position.
Press the Pressure button.
Adjust the cooking time for 60 minutes.
Once cooked, take the pork out and shred using forks.
Serve with the sauce. Enjoy!
Nutrition Values (Per Serving):
Calories: 322
Fats: 3g
Carbs: 1g
Protein: 28g

Beef Pot Roast

Preparation Time: 15 minutes
Cooking Time: 45 minutes
Servings: 6
Ingredients:
2 tbsp. vegetable oil
1 tbsp. onion powder
1 can beef broth
1 1/2 tbsp. Worcestershire sauce
1 onion, cut into wedges
4 carrots, peeled and sliced
4 large potatoes, peeled and cut into bite-sized pieces
Salt and pepper, to taste
Directions:
Press the Sear/Sauté button on the Ninja Foodi. Then press the Start button.
Heat the oil and sear the beef chuck roast for 2 minutes on each side.
Season with salt, pepper, and onion powder.
Once golden, stir in the rest of the ingredients.
Close the pressure lid and set the vent to SEAL position.
Press the Pressure button and adjust the cooking time to 60 minutes.
Press the START button and cook until done. Serve and enjoy!
Nutrition Values (Per Serving):
Calories: 543
Fats: 21g
Carbs: 3g
Protein: 33g

Bone-In Pork Chops with Veggies

Preparation Time: 5 minutes

Cooking Time: 10 minutes
Servings: 4
Ingredients:
4 3/4 inch bone-in pork chops
Salt and pepper, to taste
1/4 cup baby carrots
4 whole potatoes, peeled and halved
1 onion, chopped
1 cup vegetable broth
3 tbsp. vegetable broth
3 tbsp. Worcestershire sauce
Directions:
Season the beef with salt and pepper. Dredge in flour.
Press the Sear/Saute button and then the Start button.
Season the pork with salt and pepper, to taste.
Put half of the butter in the pot and sear the pork for at least 2 minutes on both sides.
Stir in the carrots, potatoes, onions, vegetable broth, and Worcestershire sauce.
Close the pressure lid and set the vent to SEAL.
Press the Pressure button and adjust the cooking time to 30 minutes.
Do natural pressure release.
Once the lid is open, stir in the remaining butter. Serve and enjoy!
Nutrition Values (Per Serving):
Calories: 210
Fats: 2g
Carbs: 1g
Protein: 18g

Pressure Cooked Adobo

Preparation Time: 10 minutes

Cooking Time: 40 minutes
Servings: 3
Ingredients:
1/4 cup fresh cilantro leaves
1/4 cup lime juice
2 garlic cloves
1/2 tsp. red pepper flakes
1/4 tsp. salt
1 pound pork tenderloin
3/4 cup chicken broth
1/4 cup lemon juice
Directions:
Place all ingredients in the pot except for the hard-boiled eggs.
Close the pressure lid and set the vent to SEAL.
Press the Pressure button and adjust the cooking time to 40 minutes.
Do natural pressure release. Serve and enjoy!
Nutrition Values (Per Serving):
Calories: 177
Fats: 6g
Carbs: 2g
Protein: 20g

Tex-Mex Meatloaf Recipe

Preparation Time: 15 minutes
Cooking Time: 30 minutes
Servings: 8
Ingredients:
1 lb. uncooked ground beef
1 tbsp. garlic powder
2 tsp. ground cumin
2 tsp. chili powder
1 tsp. cayenne pepper
1 egg
1 bell pepper, diced
2 tsp. kosher salt
1/4 cup fresh cilantro leaves
1/4 barbecue sauce, divided.
1/2 jalapeño pepper, seeds removed, minced
1 small onion, peeled, diced
3 corn tortillas, roughly chopped.
1 cup water
1 cup corn chips, crushed
Directions:
Stir together all the ingredients in a large mixing bowl.
Place meat mixture in the 8 ½-inch loaf pan and cover tightly with aluminum foil
Pour water into pot. Place the loaf pan on the reversible rack, making sure rack is in the lower position. Place rack with pan in pot. Assemble the pressure lid, making sure the PRESSURE RELEASE valve is in the SEAL position
Select PRESSURE and set to HIGH. Set time to 15 minutes. Select START/STOP to begin
When pressure cooking is complete, quick release the pressure by moving the PRESSURE RELEASE valve to the VENT position. Carefully remove lid when unit has finished releasing pressure
Carefully remove foil from loaf pan and close crisping lid. Select BAKE/ROAST, set temperature to 360°F, and set time to 15 minutes. Select START/STOP to begin.
While the meatloaf is cooking, stir together the crushed corn chips and 2 tbsp. barbecue sauce in a bowl.

After 7 minutes, open lid and top meatloaf with the corn chip mixture. Close lid to resume cooking. When cooking is complete, remove meatloaf from pot and allow to cool for 10 minutes before serving

Nutrition Values (Per Serving):
Calories: 156
Fats: 4g
Carbs: 2g
Protein: 12g

Lamb and Eggplant Casserole

Preparation Time: 5 minutes
Cooking Time: 20 minutes
Servings: 4
Ingredients:
1 ½ lb. lean ground lamb
1 small eggplant about 3/4 lb., stemmed and diced
8-ounces dried spiral-shaped pasta, such as rotini
1 tbsp. minced garlic
2 tbsp. olive oil
1 medium red onion, chopped.
1/2 cup canned tomato paste
3/4 cup dry red wine, such as Syrah
2 ¼ cups chicken broth
1/2 tbsp. dried oregano
1/2 tsp. dried dill
1 tsp. ground cinnamon
1/2 tsp. salt
1/2 tsp. ground black pepper
Directions:
Heat the oil in the Ninja Foodi Multi-cooker turned to the *Sauté* function. Add the onion and cook, often stirring, until softened, about 4 minutes. Add the garlic and cook until aromatic, less than 1 minute.
Crumble in the ground lamb; cook, stirring occasionally until it has lost its raw color, about 5 minutes. Add the eggplant and cook for 1 minute, often stirring, to soften a bit. Pour in the red wine and scrape up any browned bits in the pot as it comes to a simmer Stir in the broth, tomato paste, cinnamon, oregano, dill, salt and pepper until everything is coated in the tomato sauce. Stir in the pasta until coated.
High pressure for 8 minutes. Lock the lid on the Ninja Foodi Multi-cooker and then cook for 8 minutes.
To get 8 minutes' cook time, press *Pressure* button and use the Time Adjustment button to adjust the cook time to 8 minutes
Pressure Release. Use the quick release method.
Remove the lid from the Ninja Foodi Multi-cooker. Close crisping lid. Select "BROIL" and set time to 5 minutes. Cooking for an additional 4 minutes if dish needs more browning. Unlock and open the pot. Stir well before serving

Nutrition Values (Per Serving):
Calories: 244
Fats: 2g
Carbs: 5g
Protein: 30g

Beef Bites

Preparation Time: 5 minutes
Cooking Time: 10 minutes
Servings: 8
Ingredients:
1 lb. beef meat, ground
1 egg; whisked.
1 yellow onion; chopped.
3 tbsp. breadcrumbs
½ tsp. garlic; minced.
Cooking spray
Salt and black pepper to the taste
Directions:
In a bowl mix all the ingredients except the cooking spray, stir well and shape medium meatballs out of this mix
Put the meatballs in the Air Crisp basket, grease them with cooking spray, put the basket in the Foodi, set the machine on Air Crisp and cook the meatballs at 390 °F for 15 minutes.
Nutrition Values (Per Serving):
Calories: 156
Fats: 8g
Carbs: 4g
Protein: 28g

Beef Chili & Cornbread Casserole

Preparation Time: 10 minutes
Cooking Time: 50 minutes
Servings: 8
Ingredients:
2 lb. uncooked ground beef
3 cans 14-ounces each kidney beans, rinsed, drained
1 can 28-ounces crushed tomatoes
1 cup beef stock
1 large white onion, peeled, diced
1 green bell pepper, diced
1 jalapeño pepper, diced, seeds removed
4 cloves garlic, peeled, minced
2 tbsp. kosher salt
1 tbsp. ground black pepper
2 tbsp. ground cumin
1 tbsp. onion powder
1 tbsp. garlic powder
2 cups Cheddar Corn Bread batter, uncooked
1 cup shredded Mexican cheese blend
Sour cream, for serving
Directions:
Place beef, beans, tomatoes, and stock into the pot, breaking apart meat. Assemble pressure lid, making sure the PRESSURE RELEASE valve is in the SEAL position. Select PRESSURE and set to HIGH. Set time to 15 minutes. Select START/STOP to begin. When pressure cooking is complete, quick release the pressure by moving the PRESSURE RELEASE valve to the VENT position. Carefully remove lid when unit has finished releasing pressure
Select SEAR/SAUTÉ. Set temperature to MD, Select START/STOP. Add onion, green bell pepper, jalapeño pepper, garlic, and spices; stir to incorporate. Bring to a simmer and cook for 5 minutes, stirring occasionally.
Dollop corn bread batter evenly over the top of the chili. Close crisping lid. Select BAKE/ROAST, set temperature to 360°F, and set time to 26 minutes. Select START/STOP to begin.
After 15 minutes, open lid and insert a wooden toothpick into the center of the corn bread. If corn bread is not done, close lid to resume cooking for another 8 minutes

When corn bread is done, sprinkle it with cheese and close lid to resume cooking for 3 minutes, or until cheese is melted. When cooking is complete, top with sour cream and serve.

Nutrition Values (Per Serving):

Calories: 490
Fats: 4g
Carbs: 3g
Protein: 24g

Pressure Cooked Short Ribs

Preparation Time: 15 minutes
Cooking Time: 50 minutes
Servings: 8
Ingredients:
1 bottle (750 mL): red wine
4 pounds beef, short ribs
3 tbsp. unsalted butter
1 1/2 cups onion, chopped
3 garlic cloves, minced
1 cup minced carrots
2 sprigs fresh rosemary
2 cups chicken stock
Salt and pepper, to taste
Directions:
Place all ingredients in the pot except for the hard-boiled eggs.
Close the pressure lid and set the vent to SEAL.
Press the Pressure button and adjust the cooking time to 60 minutes.
Do natural pressure release.
Season with salt and pepper, to taste. Serve and enjoy!
Nutrition Values (Per Serving):
Calories: 444
Fats: 8g
Carbs: 4g
Protein: 25g

Mexican Pork in Annatto Sauce

Preparation Time: 10 minutes
Cooking Time: 1 hour 10 minutes
Servings: 10
Ingredients:
3 oz. achiote paste or annatto powder
1 white onion, chopped
2 garlic cloves, minced
2 cups orange juice
1/2 cup lemon juice
1/4 cup white vinegar
2 tbsp. salt
1 tbsp. ground black pepper
1 tbsp. Mexican oregano
5 pounds pork shoulder roast
Directions:
Place all ingredients in the Ninja Foodi Pot.
Close the pressure lid and set the vent to SEAL.
Press the Pressure button and adjust the cooking time to 75 minutes.
Do a natural pressure release. Serve and enjoy!
Nutrition Values (Per Serving):
Calories: 430
Fats: 16g
Carbs: 9g
Protein: 35g

Red Wine Braised Short Ribs

Preparation Time: 5 minutes
Cooking Time: 50 minutes
Servings: 10
Ingredients:
5 pounds beef short ribs, cut into chunks
2/3 cup all-purpose flour
2 tbsp. olive oil
2 tbsp. olive oil
2 onions, chopped
2 garlic cloves, minced
2 stalks celery, chopped
2 tbsp. tomato paste
3 carrots, peeled and sliced
4 cups beef stock
1 cup dry red wine
Salt and pepper, to taste
Directions:
First season the ribs with salt and pepper.
Dredge the meat on all-purpose flour.
Press the Sear/Saute button and then the Start button.
Heat the oil and sear the meat on all sides for at least 3 minutes.
Sauté the onion and garlic until fragrant.
Stir in the celery until wilted.
Add the rest of the ingredients.
Close the pressure lid and set the vent to SEAL.
Press the Pressure button and adjust the cooking time to 60 minutes. Serve and enjoy!
Nutrition Values (Per Serving):
Calories: 188
Fats: 8g
Carbs: 4g
Protein: 20g

Keto Corned Beef

Preparation Time: 5 minutes
Cooking Time: 13 minutes
Servings: 4
Ingredients:
1 can corned beef
1/4 green bell pepper, chopped
1/4 onion, chopped
1 tsp. vegetable oil
2 tsp. tomato paste
1/4 tsp. dried thyme
Salt and pepper, to taste
Directions:
Place the Ninja Foodi Cook and Crisp reversible rack inside the ceramic pot.
Pour water into the pot.
Place in a heat-proof dish the rest of the ingredients and then stir to combine.
Place the dish on the reversible rack.
Close the pressure lid and set the vent to SEAL.
Press the Steam button and adjust the cooking time to 15 minutes. Serve and enjoy!
Nutrition Values (Per Serving):
Calories: 211
Fats: 8g
Carbs: 4g
Protein: 21g

Keto Steamed Pork

Preparation Time: 5 minutes
Cooking Time: 40 minutes
Servings: 2
Ingredients:
2 boneless pork chops
2 tbsp. fresh orange juice
2 cups water
1/4 tsp. ground cloves
1/4 tsp. ground coriander
1/4 tsp. ground cinnamon
1 pinch cayenne pepper
Directions:
Place all ingredients in a Ziploc bag and marinate in the fridge for at least 2 hours.
Place the Ninja Foodi Cook Crisp reversible rack inside the ceramic pot.
Pour water into the pot and place the marinated meat on the reversible rack.
Close the pressure lid and set the vent to SEAL.
Press the Steam button and adjust the cooking time to 45 minutes. Serve and enjoy!
Nutrition Values (Per Serving):
Calories: 411
Fats: 12g
Carbs: 4g
Protein: 25g

Snacks and Appetizers

Kale And Almonds Mix

Preparation Time: 5 minutes
Cooking Time: 4 minutes
Servings: 4
Ingredients:
1 cup of water
1 big kale bunch, chopped
1 tablespoon balsamic vinegar
1/3 cup toasted almonds
3 garlic cloves, minced
1 small yellow onion, chopped
2 tablespoons olive oil

Directions:
Set your Ninja Foodi on Saute mode and add oil, let it heat up
Stir in onion and cook for 3 minutes. Add garlic, water, kale, and stir
Lock lid and cook on HIGH pressure for 4 minutes. Quick release pressure
Add salt, pepper, vinegar, almonds and toss well. Serve and enjoy!
Nutrition Values (Per Serving):
Calories: 189
Fats: 21g
Carbs: 4g
Protein: 32g

Simple Treat Of Garlic

Preparation Time: 10 minutes
Cooking Time: 5 minutes
Servings: 4
Ingredients:
1 tablespoon extra-virgin olive oil
2 garlic cloves, minced
2 large-sized Belgian endive, halved lengthwise
½ cup apple cider vinegar
½ cup broth
Salt and pepper to taste
1 teaspoon cayenne pepper
Directions:
Set your Ninja Foodi to Saute mode and add oil, let the oil heat up
Add garlic and cook for 30 seconds unto browned
Add endive, vinegar, broth, salt, pepper, and cayenne
Lock lid and cook on LOW pressure for 2 minutes. Quick release pressure and serve. Enjoy!
Nutrition Values (Per Serving):
Calories: 409
Fats: 21g
Carbs: 7g
Protein: 30g

Buttered Up Garlic And Fennel

Preparation Time: 10 minutes
Cooking Time: 5 minutes
Servings: 4
Ingredients:
½ stick butter
2 garlic cloves, sliced
½ teaspoon salt
1 and ½ pounds fennel bulbs, cut into wedges
¼ teaspoon ground black pepper
½ teaspoon cayenne
¼ teaspoon dried dill weed
1/3 cup dry white wine
2/3 cup stock
Directions:
Set your Ninja Foodi to Saute mode and add butter, let it heat up
Add garlic and cook for 30 seconds. Add rest of the ingredients
Lock lid and cook on LOW pressure for 3 minutes. Remove lid and serve. Enjoy!
Nutrition Values (Per Serving):
Calories: 332
Fats: 7g
Carbs: 4g
Protein: 18g

Delicious Paprika And Cabbage

Preparation Time: 10 minutes
Cooking Time: 4 minutes
Servings: 4
Ingredients:
1 and ½ pounds green cabbage, shredded
Salt and pepper to taste
3 tablespoon ghee
1 cup vegetable stock
¼ teaspoon sweet paprika
Directions:
Set your Ninja Foodi to Saute mode and add ghee, let it melt
Add cabbage, salt, pepper, and stock, stir well
Lock lid and cook on HIGH pressure for 7 minutes. Quick release pressure
Add paprika and toss well. Divide between plates and serve. Enjoy!
Nutrition Values (Per Serving):
Calories: 177
Fats: 8g
Carbs: 4g
Protein: 25g

Authentic Western Omelet

Preparation Time: 5 minutes
Cooking Time: 34 minutes
Servings: 2
Ingredients:
3 eggs, whisked
3 ounces chorizo, chopped
1-ounces Feta cheese, crumbled
5 tablespoons almond milk
¾ teaspoon chili flakes
¼ teaspoon salt
1 green pepper, chopped
Directions:
Add all the ingredients and mix them well. Stir it gently. Take an omelet pan and pour the mixture into it. Preheat your Ninja Foodi at "Roast/Bake" mode at 320 F. Cook for 4 minutes. After that, transfer the pan with an omelet in Ninja Foodi Cook for 30 minutes more at the same mode. Serve hot and enjoy!
Nutrition Values (Per Serving):
Calories: 321
Fats: 2g
Carbs: 2g
Protein: 35g

Bowl Full Of Broccoli Salad

Preparation Time: 10 minutes
Cooking Time: 5 minutes
Servings: 4
Ingredients:
1 pound broccoli, cut into florets
2 tablespoons balsamic vinegar
2 garlic cloves, minced
1 teaspoon mustard seeds
1 teaspoon cumin seeds
Salt and pepper to taste
1 cup cottage cheese, crumbled
Directions:
Add 1 cup water to your Ninja Foodi. Place steamer basket
Place broccoli in basket and lock lid, cook on HIGH pressure for 5 minutes
Quick release pressure and remove lid. Toss broccoli with other ingredients and serve. Enjoy!
Nutrition Values (Per Serving):
Calories: 540
Fats: 6g
Carbs: 2g
Protein: 12g

Rise And Shine Casserole

Preparation Time: 10 minutes
Cooking Time: 10 minutes
Servings: 2
Ingredients:
4 whole eggs
1 tablespoons milk
1 cup ham, cooked and chopped
½ cup cheddar cheese, shredded
¼ teaspoon salt
¼ teaspoon ground black pepper

Directions:
Take a baking pan (small enough to fit into your Ninja Foodi) bowl, and grease it well with butter. Take a medium bowl and whisk in eggs, milk, salt, pepper and add ham, cheese, and stir. Pour mixture into baking pan and lower the pan into your Ninja Foodi Set your Ninja Foodi Air Crisp mode and Air Crisp for 325 degrees F for 7 minutes Remove pan from eggs and enjoy!

Nutrition Values (Per Serving):
Calories: 408
Fats: 4g
Carbs: 4g
Protein: 7g

Cauliflower And Egg Dish

Preparation Time: 10 minutes
Cooking Time: 4 minutes
Servings: 4
Ingredients:
21 ounces cauliflower, separated into florets
1 cup red onion, chopped
1 cup celery, chopped
½ cup of water
Salt and pepper to taste
2 tablespoons balsamic vinegar
1 teaspoon stevia
4 boiled eggs, chopped
1 cup Keto Friendly mayonnaise
Directions:
Add water to Ninja Foodi
Add steamer basket and add cauliflower, lock lid and cook on High Pressure for 5 minutes
Quick release pressure. Transfer cauliflower to bowl and add eggs, celery, onion and toss
Take another bowl and mix in mayo, salt, pepper, vinegar, stevia and whisk well
Add a salad, toss well. Divide into salad bowls and serve. Enjoy!
Nutrition Values (Per Serving):
Calories: 510
Fats: 6g
Carbs: 4g
Protein: 10g

Just A Simple Egg Frittata

Preparation Time: 10 minutes
Cooking Time: 15 minutes
Servings: 4
Ingredients:
5 whole eggs
¾ teaspoon mixed herbs
1 cup spinach
¼ cup shredded cheddar cheese
½ cup mushrooms
Salt and pepper to taste
¾ cup half and half
2 tablespoons butter
Directions:
Dice mushrooms, chop spinach finely
Set your Ninja Foodi to Saute mode and add spinach, mushrooms
Whisk eggs, milk, cream cheese, herbs, and Sautéed vegetables in a bowl and mix well
Take a 6-inch baking pan and grease it well
Pour mixture and transfer to your Ninja Foodie (on a trivet):
Cook on HIGH pressure for 2 minutes. Quick release pressure. Serve and enjoy!
Nutrition Values (Per Serving):
Calories: 188
Fats: 4g
Carbs: 2g
Protein: 5g

Ultimate Cheese Dredged Cauliflower Snack

Preparation Time: 10 minutes
Cooking Time: 30 minutes
Servings: 4
Ingredients:
1 tablespoon mustard
1 head cauliflower
1 teaspoon avocado mayonnaise
½ cup parmesan cheese, grated
¼ cup butter, cut into small pieces
Directions:
Set your Ninja Foodi to Saute mode and add butter and cauliflower
Saute for 3 minutes. Add remaining ingredients and stir
Lock lid and cook on HIGH pressure for 30 minutes. Release pressure naturally over 10 minutes
Serve and enjoy!
Nutrition Values (Per Serving):
Calories: 187
Fats: 3g
Carbs: 4g
Protein: 6g

Quick Turkey Cutlets

Preparation Time: 10 minutes
Cooking Time: 22 minutes
Servings: 4
Ingredients:
1 teaspoon Greek seasoning
1 pound turkey cutlets
2 tablespoons olive oil
1 teaspoon turmeric powder
½ cup almond flour
Directions:
Add Greek seasoning, turmeric powder, almond flour to a bowl
Dredge turkey cutlets in it and keep it on the side for 30 minutes
Set your Foodi to Saute mode and add oil and cutlets, Saute for 2 minutes
Lock lid and cook on LOW-MEDIUM pressure for 20 minutes
Quick release pressure. Serve and enjoy!
Nutrition Values (Per Serving):
Calories: 386
Fats: 3g
Carbs: 2g
Protein: 5g

Veggies Dredged In Cheese

Preparation Time: 10 minutes
Cooking Time: 30 minutes
Servings: 4
Ingredients:
2 onions, sliced
2 tomatoes, sliced
2 zucchinis, sliced
2 teaspoons olive oil
2 cups cheddar cheese, grated
2 teaspoons mixed dried herbs
Salt and pepper to taste
Directions:
Arrange all the listed ingredients to your Ninja Foodi. Top with olive oil, herbs, cheddar, salt and pepper. Lock lid and Air Crisp for 30 minutes at 350 degrees F. Serve and enjoy!
Nutrition Values (Per Serving):
Calories: 489
Fats: 4g
Carbs: 3g
Protein: 8g

The Original Zucchini Gratin

Preparation Time: 10 minutes
Cooking Time: 15 minutes
Servings: 4
Ingredients:
2 zucchinis
1 tablespoon fresh parsley, chopped
2 tablespoons bread crumbs
4 tablespoons parmesan cheese, grated
1 tablespoon vegetable oil
Salt and pepper to taste
Directions:
Pre-heat your Ninja Foodi to 300 degrees F for 3 minutes
Slice zucchini lengthwise to get about 8 equal sizes pieces
Arrange pieces in your Crisping Basket (skin side down):
Top each with parsley, bread crumbs, cheese, oil, salt, and pepper
Return basket Ninja Foodi basket and cook for 15 minutes at 360 degrees F
Once done, serve with sauce. Enjoy!

Nutrition Values (Per Serving):

Calories: 481
Fat: 11g
Carbohydrates: 10g
Protein: 7g

Quick Bite Zucchini Fries

Preparation Time: 10 minutes
Cooking Time: 10 minutes
Servings: 4

Ingredients:
1-2 pounds of zucchini, sliced into 2 and ½ inch sticks
Salt to taste
1 cup cream cheese
2 tablespoons olive oil

Directions:
Add zucchini in a colander and season with salt, add cream cheese and mix
Add oil into your Ninja Foodie's pot and add Zucchini
Lock Air Crisping Lid and set the temperature to 365 degrees F and timer to 10 minutes
Let it cook for 10 minutes and take the dish out once done, enjoy!

Nutrition Values (Per Serving):
Calories: 374
Fat: 36g
Carbohydrates: 6g
Protein: 7g

Pickled Up Green Chili

Preparation Time: 5 minutes
Cooking Time: 11 minutes
Servings: 4

Ingredients:

1 pound green chilies
1 and ½ cups apple cider vinegar
1 teaspoon pickling salt
1 and ½ teaspoon sugar
¼ teaspoon garlic powder

Directions:

Add the listed ingredients to your pot. Lock up the lid and cook on HIGH pressure for 11 minutes. Release the pressure naturally

Spoon the mixture into jars and cover the slices with cooking liquid, making sure to completely submerge the chilies. Serve!

Nutrition Values (Per Serving):

Calories: 3
Fat: 0g
Carbohydrates: 0.8g
Protein: 0.1g

Egg Dredged Casserole

Preparation Time: 10 minutes
Cooking Time: 5 minutes
Servings: 6
Ingredients:
4 whole eggs
1 tablespoons milk
1 tomato, diced
½ cup spinach
¼ teaspoon salt
¼ teaspoon ground black pepper
Directions:
Take a baking pan (small enough to fit Ninja Foodi) and grease it with butter
Take a medium bowl and whisk in eggs, milk, salt, pepper, add veggies to the bowl and stir
Pour egg mixture into the baking pan and lower the pan into the Ninja Foodi
Close Air Crisping lid and Air Crisp for 325 degrees for 7 minutes
Remove the pan from eggs and enjoy hot!
Nutrition Values (Per Serving):
Calories: 308
Fats: 8g
Carbs: 4g
Protein: 5g

Excellent Bacon And Cheddar Frittata

Preparation Time: 10 minutes
Cooking Time: 10 minutes
Servings: 6
Ingredients:
6 whole eggs
2 tablespoons milk
½ cup bacon, cooked and chopped
1 cup broccoli, cooked
½ cup shredded cheddar cheese
¼ teaspoon salt
¼ teaspoon ground black pepper
Directions:
Take a baking pan (small enough to fit into your Ninja Foodi) bowl, and grease it well with butter. Take a medium sized bowl and add eggs, milk, salt, pepper, bacon, broccoli, and cheese. Stir well. Pour mixture into your prepared baking pan and lower pan into your Foodi, close Air Crisping lid. Air Crisp for 7 minutes at 375 degrees F. Remove pan and enjoy!
Nutrition Values (Per Serving):
Calories: 442
Fats: 5g
Carbs: 4g
Protein: 8g

Holiday And Weekend Ninja Foodie Recipes

Simple Weeknight Vanilla Yogurt

Preparation Time: 10 minutes
Cooking Time: 3 hours 0 minutes
Servings: 4
Ingredients:
½ cup full-fat milk
¼ cup yogurt started
1 cup heavy cream
½ tablespoon vanilla extract
2 teaspoons stevia
Directions:
Add milk to your Ninja Foodi and stir in heavy cream, vanilla extract, stevia
Stir well, let the yogurt sit for a while. Lock lid and cook on SLOW COOKER mode for 3 hours
Take a small bowl and add 1 cup milk with the yogurt starter, bring this mixture to the pot
Lock lid and wrap Foodi in two small towels. Let it sit for 9 hours (to allow it to culture): Refrigerate and serve. Enjoy!

Nutrition Values (Per Serving):

Calories: 292
Fat: 26g
Carbohydrates: 8g
Protein: 5g

The Great Family Lemon Mousse

Preparation Time: 10 minutes
Cooking Time: 12 minutes
Servings: 4

Ingredients:

1-2 ounces cream cheese, soft
½ cup heavy cream
1/8 cup fresh lemon juice
½ teaspoon lemon liquid stevia
2 pinch salt

Directions:

Take a bowl and mix in cream cheese, heavy cream, lemon juice, salt, and stevia
Pour mixture into a ramekin and transfer to Ninja Foodi
Lock lid and choose the Bake/Roast mode and bake for 12 minutes at 350 degrees F
Check using a toothpick if it comes out clean. Serve and enjoy!

Nutrition Values (Per Serving):

Calories: 292
Fat: 26g
Carbohydrates: 8g
Protein: 5g

Tangy Berry Slices

Preparation Time: 20 minutes
Cooking Time: 15 minutes
Servings: 4

Ingredients

1 cup cottage cheese
½ teaspoon stevia
¼ cup ground pecans
½ cup strawberries
¼ cup whipped cream
¼ cup butter

Directions:

Set your Ninja Food to Saute mode and add butter, add pecans and toss until coated
Divide mixture into 3 ramekins and press them down
Blend cheese and stevia, puree until smooth. Place cheese mixture on top of the pecan crust
Cover with fresh strawberry slices, top with whipped cream. Chill and enjoy!

Nutrition Values (Per Serving):

Calories: 200
Fat: 18g
Carbohydrates: 6g
Protein: 9g

Over The Weekend Apple And Sprouts

Preparation Time: 10 minutes

Cooking Time: 10 minutes
Servings: 4
Ingredients:
1 green apple, julienned
1 and ½ teaspoon olive oil
4 cups alfalfa sprouts
Salt and pepper to taste
¼ cup of coconut milk

Direction
Set your Ninja Foodi to Saute mode and add oil, let it heat up
Add apple, sprouts, and stir. Lock lid and cook on HIGH pressure for 5 minutes
Add salt, pepper, coconut milk and stir well. Serve3 and enjoy!

Nutrition Values (Per Serving):

Calories: 120
Fat: 3g
Carbohydrates: 3g
Protein: 3g

Generous Gluten Free Pancakes

(Prepping time: 10 minutes\ Cooking time: 16 minutes |For 4 servings):

Ingredients:

1/3 cup almond flour
½ cup of water
½ teaspoon chili powder
1 Serrano pepper, minced
4 tablespoons coconut oil
3 tablespoons coconut cream
¼ teaspoon turmeric powder
1 handful cilantro, chopped
6 large eggs
1 teaspoon salt
¼ teaspoon pepper
½ inch ginger, grated
½ red onion, chopped

Directions:

Take a bowl and add coconut milk, almond flour, spices, and blend well
Stir in ginger, Serrano, cilantro, red onion and mix
Grease interior of Ninja Foodi with coconut oil, pour batter in pot and Lock lid, cook on LOW pressure for 30 minutes. Release pressure naturally over 10 minutes
Remove pancake to a platter and serve. Enjoy!

Nutrition Values (Per Serving):

Calories: 360
Fat: 33g
Carbohydrates: 4g
Protein: 13g

Fancy Holiday Lemon Custard

Preparation Time: 10 minutes
Cooking Time: 20 minutes
Servings: 4

Ingredients:

5 egg yolks
¼ cup fresh squeezed lemon juice
1 tablespoon lemon zest
1 teaspoon pure vanilla extract
1/3 teaspoon liquid stevia
2 cups heavy cream
1 cup whipped coconut cream

Directions:

Take a medium sized bowl and whisk in yolks, lemon juice, zest, vanilla, and liquid stevia

Whisk in heavy cream, divide the mixture between 4 ramekins

Place the included rack in your Ninja Foodi and place ramekins in the rack

Add just enough water to reach halfway to the sides of the ramekins

Lock lid and cook on HIGH pressure for 20 minutes. Release pressure naturally over 10 minutes

Remove ramekins and let them cool down

Chill in fridge, top with whipped coconut cream and enjoy!

Nutrition Values (Per Serving):

Calories: 310
Fat: 30g
Carbohydrates: 3g
Protein: 7g

Gentle Peanut Butter Cheesecake

Preparation Time: 10 minutes
Cooking Time: 20 minutes
Servings: 4
Ingredients:
1/8 cup smooth peanut butter
2 whole eggs
½ teaspoon stevia
½ teaspoon vanilla extract
½ cup sour cream
2 tablespoons smooth peanut butter (additional):
Pinch of stevia
2 cups cream cheese
Directions:
Use a blender and mix in cheese, peanut butter, eggs, stevia and vanilla extract
Pour mixture in springform pan, cover with aluminum foil
Add 2 cups water to your Ninja Foodi, place pan on a trivet
Lock lid and cook on HIGH pressure for 20 minutes. Release pressure naturally over 10 minutes
Let it cool down. Add your desired toppings and spread on top. Enjoy!
Nutrition Values (Per Serving):
Calories: 480
Fat: 43g
Carbohydrates: 10g
Protein: 13g

Decisive Crème Brulee

Preparation Time: 10 minutes
Cooking Time: 20 minutes
Servings: 4
Ingredients:
1 cup heavy cream
½ tablespoon vanilla extract
3 egg yolks
1 pinch salt
¼ cup stevia
Directions:
Take a bowl and mix in egg yolks, vanilla extract, salt, and heavy cream
Mix well and beat the mixture until combined well
Divide mixture between 4 greased ramekins and evenly transfer the ramekins to your Ninja Foodi. Lock lid and select the "Bake/Roast" mode, bake for 35 minutes at 365 degrees F
Remove ramekin from Ninja Foodi and wrap with plastic wrap. Refrigerate to chill for 3 hours
Serve and enjoy!

Nutrition Values (Per Serving):

Calories: 260
Fat: 22g
Carbohydrates: 8g
Protein: 5g

The Cool Pot-De-Crème

Preparation Time: 10 minutes

Cooking Time: 20 minutes

Servings: 4

Ingredients:

6 egg yolks

2 cups heavy whip cream

1/3 cup cocoa powder

1 tablespoon pure vanilla extract

½ teaspoon liquid stevia

Whipped coconut cream for garnish

Shaved dark chocolate for garnish

Directions:

Take a medium sized bowl and whisk in yolks, heavy cream, cocoa powder, vanilla and stevia

Pour mixture in 1 and ½ quart baking dish, transfer to Nina Foodi insert

Add water to reach about half of the ramekin

Lock lid and cook on HIGH pressure for 12 minutes, quick release pressure

Remove baking dish from the insert and let it cool

Chill in fridge and serve with a garnish of coconut cream, shaved chocolate shavings. Enjoy!

Nutrition Values (Per Serving):

Calories: 257

Fat: 18g

Carbohydrates: 3g

Protein: 5g

Humming Key Lime Curd

Preparation Time: 10 minutes
Cooking Time: 10 minutes
Servings: 4
Ingredients:
3 ounces unsalted butter
1 cup liquid stevia
2 large eggs
2 large egg yolks
2/3 cup fresh key lime juice
1-2 teaspoons key lime zest
Directions:
Take food How Toor and add butter and stevia for 2 minutes
Slowly add the eggs and yolks to the processor and process to for 1 minute
Add Key Lime Juice to the blender and mix well. The mix should look curdled
Pour the mix into 3 one cup sized Mason Jars and lock up the lid
Place 1 and a ½ cups of water to your Ninja Foodi. Add the steamer basket/trivet
Place jars on the basket. Lock up the lid and cook for 10 minutes at HIGH pressure
Once done, allow the pressure to release naturally. Remove the jars and open the lids
Add Key Lime Zest to the curd and stir well. Place the lid and slightly tighten it
Cool for 20 minutes or chill in your fridge overnight. Enjoy!

Nutrition Values (Per Serving):

Calories: 60
Fat: 1g
Carbohydrates: 11g
Protein: 3g

Runny Eggs In A Cup

Preparation Time: 5 minutes
Cooking Time: 5 minutes
Servings: 4
Ingredients:
4 whole eggs
1 cup mixed veggies, diced
½ cup cheddar cheese, shredded
¼ cup half and half
Salt and pepper to taste
½ cup shredded cheese

Directions:
Take a bowl and add eggs, cheese, veggies, half and a half, pepper, salt and chop up cilantro
Mix well and divide the mix amongst four ½ a pint wide mouth mason jars (or similar containers). Slightly put the lid on top
Add 2 cups of water to your pot and place a steamer rack on top
Place the egg jars on your steamer. Lock up the lid and cook for 5 minutes at HIGH pressure
Quick release the pressure. Remove the jars and top them up with ½ a cup of cheese
Serve immediately or broil a bit to allow the cheese to melt

Nutrition Values (Per Serving):

Calories: 160
Fat: 4g
Carbohydrates: 6g
Protein: 53g

Simple Party Week Poached Pears

Preparation Time: 10 minutes
Cooking Time: 10 minutes
Servings: 6
Ingredients:
6 firm pears, peeled
1 bottle of dry red wine
1 bay leaf
4 garlic cloves, minced
1 stick cinnamon
1 fresh ginger, minced
1 and 1/3 cup stevia
Mixed Italian herbs as needed

Directions:
Peel the pears leaving the stems attached. Pour wine into your Ninja Foodi
Add bay leaf, cinnamon, cloves, ginger, stevia, and stir
Add pears to the pot and lock up the lid and cook on HIGH pressure for 9 minutes
Perform a quick release. Take the pears out using tong and keep them on the side
Set the pot to Saute mode and allow the mixture to reduce to half
Drizzle the mixture over the pears and enjoy!

Nutrition Values (Per Serving):

Protein: 0.5g
Carbs: 2g
Fats: 16g
Calories: 150

Delicious Coconut Cake

Preparation Time: 10 minutes
Cooking Time: 10 minutes
Servings: 4
Ingredients:

1 cup almond flour
½ cup unsweetened shredded coconut
1/3 cup Truvia
1 teaspoon of apple pie spice
1 teaspoon of baking powder

Wet Ingredients
¼ cup melted butter
2 lightly whisked eggs
½ cup heavy whipping cream

Directions:
Add all dry ingredients in a bowl and add the wet ingredients one at a time, making sure to gently stir after each addition. Empty batter into a pan and cover with foil
Add water 1-2 cups of water to Ninja Foodi, place steamer rack
Place pan in a steamer rack and lock lid. Cook on HIGH pressure for 40 minutes
Naturally, release pressure over 10 minutes. Quick release pressure
Remove pan and let it cool for 15-20 minutes. Flip it over onto a platter and garnish as needed
Serve and enjoy!

Nutrition Values (Per Serving):
Calories: 236
Fat: 23g
Carbohydrates: 3g
Protein: 5g

Uniform Dark Chocolate Cake

Preparation Time: 10 minutes

Cooking Time: 3 hours 10 minutes

Servings: 4

Ingredients:

1 cup + 2 tablespoons almond flour
1 and ½ teaspoons baking powder
½ cup of cocoa powder
½ cup granular swerve
3 tablespoons unflavored whey powder/egg white protein powder
¼ teaspoon salt
2/3 cup almond milk, unsweetened
3 large whole eggs
¾ teaspoon vanilla extract
6 tablespoons melted butter
1/3 cup chocolate chips, sugar-free

Directions:

Prepare a six quart Ninja Foodi and grease with oil
Add whey protein powder, almond flour, sweetener, baking powder, salt, cocoa powder
Fold in butter, eggs, vanilla extract, milk and mix well. Stir in chips and pour batter into the pot
Lock lid and SLOW COOK (HIGH) for 3 hours until a toothpick comes out clean from the center
Remove heat and let it cool for 20 minutes, slice and serve. Enjoy!

Nutrition Values (Per Serving):

Calories: 205
Fat: 17g
Carbohydrates: 9g
Protein: 8g

Side Dish

Carrot Fries

Prep + Cooking Time: 25 minutes, Servings: 4

Ingredients:

4 mixed carrots cut into sticks
2 garlic cloves; minced.
2 tbsp. rosemary; chopped.
2 tbsp. olive oil
Salt and black pepper to the taste

Directions:

In a bowl mix all the ingredients and toss them. Put the carrots in the Air Crisp basket and put the basket in the Foodi
Set the machine on Air Crisp and cook the fries at 380 °F for 15 minutes. Divide the carrot fries between plates and serve as a side dish.

Nutrition Values (Per Serving):

Calories: 337
Fats: 4g
Carbs: 2g
Protein: 15g

Brussels Sprouts

Preparation Time: 5 minutes
Cooking Time: 25 minutes
Servings: 8
Ingredients:
3 lbs. Brussels sprouts, trimmed
1 lb. bacon; chopped.
1 yellow onion; chopped.
2 cups heavy cream
4 tbsp. butter, melted
1 tsp. olive oil
Salt and black pepper to the taste
Directions:
Put the Brussels sprouts in your Foodi's Air Crisp basket and put the basket in the machine
Set it on Air Crisp and cook at 370 °F for 10 minutes. Clean the Foodi and put the sprouts in a bowl. Set the machine on Sauté mode, add the oil and the butter and heat it up
Return the Sprouts to the pot, also add the bacon and the onion, stir and cook for 5 more minutes. Add the cream, toss, cook or another 5 minutes, divide between plates and as a side dish.
Nutrition Values (Per Serving):
Calories: 654
Fats: 1g
Carbs: 1g
Protein: 2g

Asian Style Chickpeas

Preparation Time: 10 minutes
Cooking Time: 20 minutes
Servings: 4
Ingredients:
30 oz. canned chickpeas; drained.
2 tbsp. olive oil
2 tsp. garam masala
¼ tsp. mustard powder
½ tsp. garlic powder
1 tsp. sweet paprika
A pinch of salt and black pepper
Directions:
In a bowl combine all the ingredients and toss them well. Set the Ninja Foodi on Sauté mode, heat it up for 3 minutes and add the chickpeas and sauté them for 6 minutes Transfer them to the Foodi's basket, place the basket in the pot, set it on Air Crisp and cook at 400 °F for 15 minutes. Divide the chickpeas between plates and serve as a side dish
Nutrition Values (Per Serving):
Calories: 122
Fats: 1g
Carbs: 2g
Protein: 2g

Bacon and Brussels Sprouts

Preparation Time: 5 minutes
Cooking Time: 20 minutes
Servings: 4
Ingredients:
1 lb. Brussels sprouts, halved
4 bacon strips, cooked and chopped
1 tbsp. olive oil
2 tsp. garlic powder
A pinch of salt and black pepper
Directions:
In a bowl combine all the ingredients except the bacon and toss. Put the Brussels sprouts in the machine's basket, place the basket inside, set the Foodi on Air Crisp and cook at 390 °F for 20 minutes
Divide the Brussels sprouts between plates, sprinkle the bacon on top and serve.
Nutrition Values (Per Serving):
Calories: 211
Fats: 2g
Carbs: 1g
Protein: 1g

Sweet Potato Mash

Preparation Time: 5 minutes
Cooking Time: 25 minutes
Servings: 4
Ingredients:
1 ½ lbs. sweet potatoes, peeled and cubed
1 cup chicken stock
1 tbsp. honey
1 tbsp. butter, soft
Salt and black pepper to the taste
Directions:
In your Foodi, mix the sweet potatoes with the stock, salt and pepper, put the pressure lid on and cook on High for 15 minutes. Release the pressure naturally for 10 minutes
 Mash the potatoes, add the butter and the honey, whisk well, divide between plates and serve as a side dish.
Nutrition Values (Per Serving):
Calories: 127
Fats: 1g
Carbs: 2g
Protein: 2g

Oregano Potatoes

Preparation Time: 5 minutes
Cooking Time: 25 minutes
Servings: 2
Ingredients:
4 gold potatoes, cut into wedges
4 garlic cloves; minced.
½ cup water
2 tbsp. olive oil
1 tbsp. oregano; chopped.
Juice of 1 lemon
A pinch of salt and black pepper
Directions:
Put the water in the Foodi machine, add the basket and put the potatoes in it. Put the pressure lid on, set the pot on Low and cook for 4 minutes
Release the pressure naturally for 10 minutes, drain the potatoes and put them in a bowl. Clean the pot, set it on Sauté mode, add the oil and heat it up
Add the potatoes and the rest of the ingredients, toss, set the machine on Roast and cook at 400 °F for 20 minutes. Divide the potatoes between plates and serve.
Nutrition Values (Per Serving):
Calories: 127
Fats: 4g
Carbs: 1g
Protein: 2g

Carrot Puree

Preparation Time: 5 minutes
Cooking Time: 10 minutes
Servings: 4
Ingredients:
1 lb. carrots, peeled and halved
1 yellow onion; chopped.
½ cup chicken stock
¼ cup heavy cream
Salt and black pepper to the taste
Directions:
In your Foodi, combine all the ingredients except the cream, put the pressure lid on and cook on High for 15 minutes. Release the pressure naturally for 10 minutes
Mash everything well, add the cream, whisk really well, divide between plates and serve as a side dish.
Nutrition Values (Per Serving):
Calories: 224
Fats: 2g
Carbs: 1g
Protein: 4g

Baked Mushrooms

Preparation Time: 5 minutes
Cooking Time: 20 minutes
Servings: 4
Ingredients:
1 lb. white mushrooms, halved
1 tbsp. oregano; chopped.
2 tbsp. mozzarella cheese; grated.
2 tbsp. olive oil
1 tbsp. parsley; chopped.
1 tbsp. rosemary; chopped.
Salt and black pepper to the taste
Directions:
Set the Foodi on sauté mode, add the oil, heat it up and then combine all the ingredients except the cheese.
Sprinkle the cheese on top, set the machine on Baking mode and cook the mushrooms at 380 °F for 15 minutes. Divide the mushrooms between plates and serve as a side dish
Nutrition Values (Per Serving):
Calories: 435
Fats: 3g
Carbs: 1g
Protein: 1g

Roasted Potatoes

Preparation Time: 10 minutes
Cooking Time: 25 minutes
Servings: 4
Ingredients:
1 lb. baby potatoes, halved
½ cup parsley; chopped.
½ cup mayonnaise
2 tbsp. tomato paste
2 tbsp. olive oil
1 tbsp. smoked paprika
1 tbsp. garlic powder
2 tbsp. white wine vinegar
3 tsp. hot paprika
A pinch of salt and black pepper
Directions:
In a bowl combine the potatoes with the paprika, oil, smoked paprika, garlic powder, salt and pepper and toss. Put the potatoes in the basket and place the basket in the Foodi Set the machine on Air Crisp, cook the potatoes for 25 minutes at 360 °F, transfer them to a bowl, mix with the tomato paste, mayo, vinegar and the parsley, toss and serve as a side dish.
Nutrition Values (Per Serving):
Calories: 405
Fats: 8g
Carbs: 4g
Protein: 2g

Cauliflower Risotto

Preparation Time: 15 minutes
Cooking Time: 22 minutes
Servings: 4
Ingredients:
1 cauliflower head, riced
15 oz. water chestnuts; drained.
1 egg; whisked.
1 tbsp. ginger; grated.
1 tbsp. lemon juice
2 tbsp. olive oil
4 tbsp. soy sauce
3 garlic cloves; minced.

Directions:
Set the Foodi on Sauté mode, add the oil and heat it up. Add the garlic and the cauliflower rice, toss and cook for 2-3 minutes

Add the soy sauce, chestnuts and the ginger, toss, put the pressure lid on and cook on High for 15 minutes.

Release the pressure fast for 5 minutes, set the machine on Sauté mode again, add the egg, stir well and cook for 2 more minutes. Divide between plates and serve as a side dish.

Nutrition Values (Per Serving):
Calories: 437
Fats: 2g
Carbs: 4g
Protein: 2g

Paprika Beets

Preparation Time: 5 minutes
Cooking Time: 40 minutes
Servings: 4
Ingredients:
2 lbs. small beets, trimmed and halved
1 tbsp. olive oil
4 tbsp. sweet paprika
Directions:
In a bowl combine all the ingredients and toss them. Put the beets in your Air Crisp basket and put the basket in the Foodi
Set on Air Crisp and cook the beets at 380 °F for 35 minutes. Divide the beets between plates and serve as a side dish.
Nutrition Values (Per Serving):
Calories: 309
Fats: 2g
Carbs: 2g
Protein: 1g

Creamy Artichokes

Preparation Time: 5 minutes
Cooking Time: 10 minutes
Servings: 4
Ingredients:
15 oz. canned artichoke hearts, roughly
1 ½ tbsp. thyme; chopped.
2 garlic cloves; minced.
1 yellow onion; chopped.
1 cup heavy cream
1 tbsp. olive oil
1 tbsp. parmesan; grated.
Salt and black pepper to the taste
Directions:
Set the Foodi on Sauté mode, add the oil, heat it up, add the onion and the garlic, stir and sauté for 5 minutes. Add all the other ingredients except the thyme and the parmesan, toss, set the machine on Baking mode and cook at 370 °F for 15 minutes
Sprinkle the parmesan and the thyme, bake the artichokes mix for 5 more minutes, divide everything between plates and serve.
Nutrition Values (Per Serving):
Calories: 179
Fats: 3g
Carbs: 1g
Protein: 1g

Broccoli Mash

Preparation Time: 6 minutes
Cooking Time: 21 minutes
Servings: 4
Ingredients:
1 broccoli head, florets separated and steamed
½ cups veggie stock
½ tsp. turmeric powder
1 tbsp. olive oil
1 tbsp. chives; chopped.
1 tbsp. butter, melted
Salt and black pepper to the taste
Directions:
Set the Foodi on Sauté mode, add the oil, heat it up, add the broccoli florets and cook them for 4 minutes. Add all the other ingredients except the butter and the chives, put the pressure lid on and cook on High for 12 minutes
Release the pressure naturally for 10 minutes, mash the broccoli, add the butter and the chives, whisk everything well, divide between plates and serve.
Nutrition Values (Per Serving):
Calories: 208
Fats: 2g
Carbs: 1g
Protein: 2g

Cumin Green Beans

Preparation Time: 10 minutes
Cooking Time: 30 minutes
Servings: 6
Ingredients:
1 lb. green beans, trimmed
2 garlic cloves; minced.
1 tbsp. olive oil
½ tsp. cumin seeds
Salt and black pepper to the taste
Directions:
In a bowl combine all the ingredients and toss well. Put the green beans in the Air Crisp basket and put the basket in the Foodi
Set the machine on Air Crisp, cook the green beans at 370 °F for 15 minutes, divide between plates and serve as a side dish.
Nutrition Values (Per Serving):
Calories: 307
Fats: 2g
Carbs: 2g
Protein: 1g

Lemony Carrots

Preparation Time: 5 minutes
Cooking Time: 20 minutes
Servings: 2
Ingredients:
1 lb. baby carrots, trimmed
2 tsp. olive oil
2 tsp. sweet paprika
Juice of 2 lemons
Salt and black pepper to the taste
Directions:
In a bowl combine all the ingredients and toss them well. Put the carrots in the Air Crisp basket and place it in the Foodi
Set the machine on Air Crisp, cook at 400 °F for 15 minutes, divide between plates and serve as a side dish.
Nutrition Values (Per Serving):
Calories: 123
Fats: 6g
Carbs: 2g
Protein: 2g

Cauliflower Mix

Preparation Time: 10 minutes
Cooking Time: 20 minutes
Servings: 4
Ingredients:
1 ½ cup white cauliflower, florets separated
1 ½ cups purple cauliflower, florets separated
2 garlic cloves; minced.
½ cup peas
1 carrot; cubed.
2 spring onions; chopped.
2 and ½ tbsp. soy sauce
2 tbsp. olive oil
A pinch of salt and black pepper
Directions:
Set the Foodi on Sauté mode, add the oil and heat it up. Add the spring onions and garlic, stir and cook for 2-3 minutes
Add the carrots, all the cauliflower, soy sauce, salt, pepper and the peas, toss, put the pressure lid on and cook on High for 8 minutes. Release the pressure naturally for 10 minutes, divide everything between plates and serve as a side dish
Nutrition Values (Per Serving):
Calories: 211
Fats: 5g
Carbs: 2g
Protein: 1g

Potato Salad

Preparation Time: 10 minutes
Cooking Time: 20 minutes
Servings: 2
Ingredients:
2 lbs. red potatoes, scrubbed
1 yellow onion; chopped.
5 bacon strips; chopped.
2 celery stalks; chopped.
¼ cup apple cider vinegar
1 cup sauerkraut
½ cup scallions; chopped.
½ cup water
1 tbsp. mustard
¼ tsp. sweet paprika
1 tsp. sugar
A pinch of salt and black pepper
Directions:
Put the potatoes and the water in your Foodi, put the pressure lid on and cook on High for 5 minutes and release the pressure naturally for 10 minutes.
Cool down the potatoes, peel and cut into cubes. Clean the Foodi, set it on Sauté mode, add the bacon, stir and cook for 5 minutes.
Add the onion, stir and cook for another 5 minutes. Add the vinegar, toss and cook for 1 more minute.
Add the potatoes and all the other ingredients, toss, cook for a couple more minutes, divide everything between plates and serve as a side dish.
Nutrition Values (Per Serving):
Calories: 234
Fats: 2g
Carbs: 1g
Protein: 1g

Zucchini Spaghetti

Preparation Time: 5 minutes
Cooking Time: 10 minutes
Servings: 4
Ingredients:
3 zucchinis, cut with a spiralizer
1 cup sweet peas
1 cup cherry tomatoes, halved
6 basil leaves, torn
1 tbsp. olive oil
A pinch of salt and black pepper
For the pesto:
1/3 cup pine nuts
¼ cup parmesan; grated.
½ cup olive oil
3 cups basil leaves
2 garlic cloves
A pinch of salt and black pepper
Directions:
In a blender, mix ½ cup oil with 3 cups basil, garlic, pine nuts, parmesan, salt and pepper and pulse well. Set the Foodi on Sauté mode, add 1 tbsp. oil and heat it up
Add the zucchini spaghetti, peas, tomatoes and the pesto, toss, put the pressure lid on and cook on High for 5 minutes. Release the pressure fast for 5 minutes, add the torn basil leaves, toss, divide everything between plates and serve as a side dish
Nutrition Values (Per Serving):
Calories: 123
Fats: 4g
Carbs: 2g
Protein: 2g

Garlicky Broccoli

Preparation Time: 5 minutes
Cooking Time: 25 minutes
Servings: 4
Ingredients:
1 broccoli head, florets separated
3 garlic cloves; minced.
2 tbsp. lemon juice
2 tbsp. parsley; chopped.
1 tbsp. olive oil
Directions:
Set the Foodi on Sauté mode, add the oil and heat it up. Add the garlic, broccoli and lemon juice, toss and cook for 2 minutes
Put the pressure lid on, set the machine on High and cook for 15 minutes. Release the pressure naturally for 10 minutes, divide between plates and serve as a side dish.
Nutrition Values (Per Serving):
Calories: 311
Fats: 2g
Carbs: 1g
Protein: 1g

Desserts

Strawberry Cake

Preparation Time: 15 minutes
Cooking Time: 25 minutes
Servings: 6
Ingredients:
8 Tbsp butter
½ cup Baking Stevia
1 egg
1 tsp vanilla
2 cups almond flour
2 tsp baking powder
1 tsp salt
1 cup chopped strawberries
½ cup buttermilk
Directions:
Use an electric mixer to cream the butter and stevia together until they are light and fluffy.
Mix the vanilla and eggs in a small bowl then add to the mixer with the butter blend. Ix until just combined.
In a separate bowl, toss the raspberries and ¼ cup almond flour to coat the berries.
Add the remaining dry ingredients to the mixer and fold together by hand. Add the buttermilk and mix until smooth.
Add the Strawberries to the batter and mix briefly.
Pour the cake batter into your Ninja Foodi and place the lid on.
Press the air crisp button and set the temperature to 350 degrees and program the timer to 25 minutes.
Once cooked, a toothpick should come out of the center of the cake cleanly. Allow to cool and serve.
Nutrition Values (Per Serving):
Calories: 217
Fats: 21g
Carbs: 4g
Protein: 5g

Balsamic Roasted Strawberries

Preparation Time: 5 minutes
Cooking Time: 10 minutes
Servings: 4
Ingredients:
4 Cups whole Strawberries
½ cup balsamic vinegar
2 Tbsp stevia
Directions:
Place all the ingredients into the pot of the Ninja Foodi and close the crisper lid.
Press the air crisp button and set the temperature to 350 degrees and program the timer to 10 minutes.
Serve hot or chilled
Nutrition Values (Per Serving):
Calories: 187
Fats: 8g
Carbs: 4g
Protein: 2g

Almond Cake

Preparation Time: 15 minutes
Cooking Time: 25 minutes
Servings: 8
Ingredients:
8 Tbsp butter
½ cup Baking Stevia
1 egg
1 tsp vanilla
2 cups almond flour
2 tsp baking powder
1 tsp salt
1 cup chopped Almonds
½ cup buttermilk

Directions:
Use an electric mixer to cream the butter and stevia together until they are light and fluffy.
Mix the vanilla and eggs in a small bowl then add to the mixer with the butter blend until just combined
Add the remaining dry ingredients to the mixer and fold together by hand. Add the buttermilk and mix until smooth.
Add the almonds to the batter and mix briefly.
Pour the cake batter into your Ninja Foodi and place the lid on.
Press the air crisp button and set the temperature to 350 degrees and program the timer to 25 minutes.
Once cooked, a toothpick should come out of the center of the cake cleanly. Allow to cool and serve.

Nutrition Values (Per Serving):
Calories: 295
Fats: 29g
Carbs: 6g
Protein: 7g

Creative Almond And Carrot Cake

Preparation Time: 10 minutes
Cooking Time: 50 minutes
Servings: 4
Ingredients:
3 whole eggs
1 cup almond flour
2/3 cup Swerve
1 teaspoon baking powder
1 and ½ teaspoons apple pie spice
¼ cup of coconut oil
½ cup heavy whip cream (Keto friendly):
1 cup carrots, shredded
½ cup walnuts, chopped
Directions:
Take a 6-inch pan and grease it up well
Take a bowl and add all of the listed ingredients, mix them well until you have a nice and fluffy mix. Use a hand mixer if needed. Pour the batter into your pan and cover with a foil
Place a steamer rack/trivet on top of your Ninja Foodi
Add 2 cups of water and transfer the pan to the rack
Lock up the lid and cook for 40 minutes on BAKE mode at 350 degrees F
Once done, release the pressure naturally over 10 minutes
Enjoy the cake as it is or if you want, then add some Keto friendly frosting/toppings
Nutrition Values (Per Serving):
Calories: 190
Fats: 188g
Carbs: 4g
Protein: 5g

Key Lime Curd

Preparation Time: 10 minutes
Cooking Time: 10 minutes
Servings: 6
Ingredients:
3 oz butter
½ cup baking stevia
2 eggs
2 egg yolks
2/3 cup key lime juice
2 tsp lime zest
Directions:
Blend the butter and stevia then add in the eggs slowly, creating an emulsion.
Add the key lime juice and zest and the separate into mason jars.
Add 1 ½ cups of water to the bottom of the Ninja Foodi and place the mason jars on top of the metal trivet inside the pot.
Place the pressure cooker lid on the pot and set the pressure cooker function to high pressure for 10 minutes. Let the pressure release naturally after the cooking time is completed.
Let cool and then enjoy.
Nutrition Values (Per Serving):
Calories: 157
Fats: 15g
Carbs: 3g
Protein: 3g

Chocolate Cheese Cake

Preparation Time: 15 minutes
Cooking Time: 20 minutes
Servings: 6
Ingredients:
Crust: ¼ cup almond flour
¼ cup coconut flour
2 Tbsp stevia
2 Tbsp melted butter
Filling: 16 oz cream cheese
½ cup baking stevia
1/3 cup cocoa powder
1 egg and 2 egg yolks
¼ cup sour cream
¾ cup heavy cream
6 oz melted chocolate
1 tsp vanilla
Directions:
In a small bowl, mix all the ingredients for the crust together. Press the crust into a 7" spring form pan wrapped in foil. Set aside.

Add the cream cheese, stevia and cocoa powder to a food processor and blend. Add the egg and yolks and blend again. Add remaining ingredients and mix just to combine. Pour cheesecake mix on top of the prepared crust.

Place the pan in the Ninja Foodi bowl on top of the metal trivet. Add 2 cups of water to the bowl under the cake. Place the pressure cooker lid on and set it to high pressure for 20 minutes. Allow the pot to naturally release the pressure once he cooking time is done. Chill and then serve.

Nutrition Values (Per Serving):
Calories: 332
Fats: 1g
Carbs: 2g
Protein: 2g

Lemon Ricotta Cake

Preparation Time: 15 minutes
Cooking Time: 20 minutes
Servings: 6
Ingredients:
Crust: ¼ cup almond flour
¼ cup coconut flour
2 Tbsp stevia
2 Tbsp melted butter
Filling: 8 oz cream cheese
½ cup baking stevia
8 ounces ricotta
1 egg and 2 egg yolks
¼ cup sour cream
¾ cup heavy cream
2 Tsp lemon zest
1 tsp vanilla

Directions:
In a small bowl, mix all the ingredients for the crust together. Press the crust into a 7" spring form pan wrapped in foil. Set aside.

Add the cream cheese, stevia and ricotta to a food processor and blend. Add the egg and yolks and blend again. Add remaining ingredients and mix just to combine. Pour cheesecake mix on top of the prepared crust.

Place the pan in the Ninja Foodi bowl on top of the metal trivet. Add 2 cups of water to the bowl under the cake. Place the pressure cooker lid on and set it to high pressure for 20 minutes. Allow the pot to naturally release the pressure once he cooking time is done. Chill and then serve.

Nutrition Values (Per Serving):
Calories: 546
Fats: 3g
Carbs: 2g
Protein: 2g

Lemon Mousse

Preparation Time: 10 minutes
Cooking Time: 12 minutes
Servings: 4
Ingredients:
1-2 ounces cream cheese, soft
½ cup heavy cream
1/8 cup fresh lemon juice
½ teaspoon lemon liquid stevia
2 pinch salt
Directions:
Take a bowl and mix in cream cheese, heavy cream, lemon juice, salt, and stevia
Pour mixture into a ramekin and transfer to Ninja Foodi
Lock lid and choose the Bake/Roast mode and bake for 12 minutes at 350 degrees F
Check using a toothpick if it comes out clean. Serve and enjoy!
Nutrition Values (Per Serving):
Calories: 478
Fats: 2g
Carbs: 0g
Protein: 1g

Tangy Berry Slices

Preparation Time: 20 minutes
Cooking Time: 15 minutes
Servings: 4
Ingredients:
1 cup cottage cheese
½ teaspoon stevia
¼ cup ground pecans
½ cup strawberries
¼ cup whipped cream
¼ cup butter
Directions:
Set your Ninja Food to Saute mode and add butter, add pecans and toss until coated
Divide mixture into 3 ramekins and press them down.
Blend cheese and stevia, puree until smooth. Place cheese mixture on top of the pecan crust
Cover with fresh strawberry slices, top with whipped cream. Chill and enjoy!
Nutrition Values (Per Serving):
Calories: 210
Fats: 9g
Carbs: 2g
Protein: 1g

Almond Cheese Cake

Preparation Time: 15 minutes
Cooking Time: 20 minutes
Servings: 6
Ingredients:
Crust: ½ cup almond flour
2 Tbsp stevia
2 Tbsp melted butter
Filling: 16 oz cream cheese
½ cup baking stevia
1 egg
2 egg yolks
¼ cup sour cream
¾ cup heavy cream
1 tsp almond extract
Directions:
In a small bowl, mix all the ingredients for the crust together. Press the crust into a 7" spring form pan wrapped in foil. Set aside.
Add the cream cheese, stevia and cocoa powder to a food processor and blend. Add the egg and yolks and blend again. Add remaining ingredients and mix just to combine. Pour cheesecake mix on top of the prepared crust.
Place the pan in the Ninja Foodi bowl on top of the metal trivet. Add 2 cups of water to the bowl under the cake. Place the pressure cooker lid on and set it to high pressure for 20 minutes. Allow the pot to naturally release the pressure once he cooking time is done. Chill and then serve.
Nutrition Values (Per Serving):
Calories: 198
Fats: 2g
Carbs: 3g
Protein: 2g

Cinnamon Pears

Preparation Time: 10 minutes
Cooking Time: 15 minutes
Servings: 4
Ingredients:
4 pears, cored and cut into wedges
¼ cup brown sugar
1 tbsp. maple syrup
4 tbsp. butter, melted
2 tsp. cinnamon powder
Directions:
In your Foodi's baking pan, combine all the ingredients and toss. Put the reversible rack into the Foodi, put the baking pan inside, set the machine on Baking mode and cook at 360 °F for 15 minutes. Divide between dessert plates and serve
Nutrition Values (Per Serving):
Calories: 612
Fats: 8g
Carbs: 4g
Protein: 2g

Apple Bread

Preparation Time: 10 minutes
Cooking Time: 40 minutes
Servings: 6
Ingredients:
3 apples, peeled and pureed
2 eggs; whisked.
2 cups white flour
1 cup sugar
1 stick of butter, melted
1 tbsp. baking powder
<u>Directions:</u>
In a bowl mix all the ingredients and whisk well. Pour this into a loaf pan that fits the Foodi. Put the reversible rack in the Foodi, put the loaf pan inside, set the machine on Baking mode and cook at 340 °F for 40 minutes. Cool the sweet bread down, slice and serve.
<u>Nutrition Values (Per Serving):</u>
Calories: 127
Fats: 2g
Carbs: 4g
Protein: 1g

Apple Pudding

Preparation Time: 5 minutes
Cooking Time: 10 minutes
Servings: 6
Ingredients:
4 apples, peeled, cored and pureed
1 cup milk
1 cup maple syrup
2 eggs; whisked.
1 tbsp. cornstarch
1 tsp. cinnamon powder
Directions:
In a bowl mix all the ingredients, whisk and divide into 6 ramekins. Put the reversible rack in the Foodi, put the ramekins inside, set the machine on Baking mode and cook at 340 °F for 25 minutes. Serve the pudding warm.
Nutrition Values (Per Serving):
Calories: 154
Fats: 4g
Carbs: 6g
Protein: 18g

Easy Cake

Preparation Time: 10 minutes
Cooking Time: 40 minutes
Servings: 6
Ingredients:
2 eggs; whisked.
1 cup ricotta cheese, soft
¼ cup walnuts; chopped.
1 cup white flour
½ cup sugar
½ cup cocoa powder
3 tbsp. butter, melted
2 tsp. baking powder
Directions:
In a bowl mix all the ingredients and whisk well. Pour the mix into the Foodi's cake pan and put the pan in the machine on the reversible rack
Set the Foodi on Baking mode, cook the cake at 320 °F for 40 minutes, cool down, slice and serve.
Nutrition Values (Per Serving):
Calories: 204
Fats: 2g
Carbs: 1g
Protein: 2g

Blackberries Cream

Preparation Time: 10 minutes
Cooking Time: 20 minutes
Servings: 4
Ingredients:
8 oz. cream cheese
4 oz. blackberries.
½ cup heavy cream
½ tbsp. lime juice
2 tbsp. water
¼ tsp. sugar
Directions:
In your blender, mix all the ingredients, pulse well and divide into 4 ramekins. Put the reversible rack in the Foodi, put the ramekins inside, set the machine on Baking mode and cook at 340 °F for 15 minutes. Serve the cream cold.
Nutrition Values (Per Serving):
Calories: 489
Fats: 1g
Carbs: 1g
Protein: 3g

Graham Cheesecake

Preparation Time: 10 minutes
Cooking Time: 25 minutes
Servings: 8
Ingredients:
1 lb. cream cheese, soft
1 cup graham cookies, crumbled
2 eggs; whisked.
4 tbsp. brown sugar
2 tbsp. butter, melted
½ tsp. vanilla extract
Cooking spray
Directions:
In a bowl mix the cookies with the butter and press this on the bottom of a cake pan greased with cooking spray. In a bowl mix all the other ingredients, stir well and pour over the graham cookie crust

Put the reversible rack in the Foodi, put the cake pan inside, set the machine on Baking mode and cook at 320 °F 15 minutes. Keep the cheesecake in the fridge for a few hours before serving.

Nutrition Values (Per Serving):
Calories: 331
Fats: 2g
Carbs: 1g
Protein: 2g

Raspberry Mug Cake

Preparation Time: 5 minutes
Cooking Time: 5 minutes
Servings: 2
Ingredients:
2/3 cup almond flour
2 eggs
2 Tbsp maple syrup
1 tsp vanilla
1/8 tsp salt
1 cup fresh raspberries
Directions:
Mix all the ingredients together except the raspberries. Fold well to ensure no lumps. Fold in raspberries.

Pour the batter into two 8 oz mason jars and cover the jars with foil.

Place the metal trivet into the Ninja Foodi and add 1 cup of water to the bowl.

Place the two mason jars on top of the trivet and close the pressure cooker top. Seal the steamer valve and set the timer to 10 minutes.

Let the pressure naturally release and then open the lid and enjoy the warm cake.

Nutrition Values (Per Serving):
Calories: 215
Fats: 2g
Carbs: 1g
Protein: 2g

Strawberry Chocolate Chip Mug Cake

Preparation Time: 5 minutes
Cooking Time: 10 minutes
Servings: 2
Ingredients:
2/3 cup almond flour
2 eggs
2 Tbsp maple syrup
1 tsp vanilla
1/8 tsp salt
½ cup chopped strawberries
¼ cup dark chocolate chips
Directions:
Mix all the ingredients together except the strawberries and chocolate chips. Fold well to ensure no lumps.
Fold in strawberries and chocolate chips.
Pour the batter into two 8 oz mason jars and cover the jars with foil.
Place the metal trivet into the Ninja Foodi and add 1 cup of water to the bowl.
Place the two mason jars on top of the trivet and close the pressure cooker top. Seal the steamer valve and set the timer to 10 minutes
Let the pressure naturally release and then open the lid and enjoy the warm cake.
Nutrition Values (Per Serving):
Calories: 153
Fats: 2g
Carbs: 4g
Protein: 2g

Chocolate Mug Cake

Preparation Time: 5 minutes
Cooking Time: 10 minutes
Servings: 2
Ingredients:
2/3 cup almond flour
¼ cup cocoa powder
2 eggs
2 Tbsp maple syrup
1 tsp vanilla
¼ tsp salt
Directions:
Mix all the ingredients together. Fold well to ensure no lumps.
Pour the batter into two 8 oz mason jars and cover the jars with foil.
Place the metal trivet into the Ninja Foodi and add 1 cup of water to the bowl.
Place the two mason jars on top of the trivet and close the pressure cooker top. Seal the steamer valve and set the timer to 10 minutes
Let the pressure naturally release and then open the lid and enjoy the warm cake.
Nutrition Values (Per Serving):
Calories: 186
Fats: 2g
Carbs: 2g
Protein: 2g

Coconut Cake

Preparation Time: 15 minutes
Cooking Time: 25 minutes
Servings: 6
Ingredients:
8 Tbsp butter
½ cup Baking Stevia
1 egg
1 tsp vanilla
1 cup coconut flour
½ cup almond flour
½ cup shredded coconut, unsweetened
2 tsp baking powder
1 tsp salt
1 cup chopped strawberries
½ cup buttermilk
Directions:
Use an electric mixer to cream the butter and stevia together until they are light and fluffy.
Mix the vanilla and eggs in a small bowl then add to the mixer with the butter blend until just combined
Add the remaining dry ingredients to the mixer and fold together by hand. Add the buttermilk and mix until smooth.
Pour the cake batter into your Ninja Foodi and place the lid on.
Press the air crisp button and set the temperature to 350 degrees and program the timer to 25 minutes.
Once cooked, a toothpick should come out of the center of the cake cleanly. Allow to cool and serve.
Nutrition Values (Per Serving):
Calories: 191
Fats: 18g
Carbs: 6g
Protein: 3g

Carrot Pecan

Preparation Time: 15 minutes
Cooking Time: 25 minutes
Servings: 2
Ingredients:
8 Tbsp butter
½ cup Baking Stevia
1 egg
1 tsp vanilla
1 cup almond flour
1 cup pecan flour
1 cup shredded carrots
2 tsp baking powder
1 tsp salt
¼ cup buttermilk

Directions:
Use an electric mixer to cream the butter and stevia together until they are light and fluffy.
Mix the vanilla and eggs in a small bowl then add to the mixer with the butter blend until just combined
Add the remaining dry ingredients to the mixer and fold together by hand. Add the buttermilk and mix until smooth.
Pour the cake batter into your Ninja Foodi and place the lid on.
Press the air crisp button and set the temperature to 350 degrees and program the timer to 25 minutes.
Once cooked, a toothpick should come out of the center of the cake cleanly. Allow to cool and serve.

Nutrition Values (Per Serving):
Calories: 198
Fats: 2g
Carbs: 1g
Protein: 1g

Grocery List

Produce:
- Cabbage
- Mushroom
- Rice
- Onions
- Pepper
- Lettuce
- Tomatoes
- Lemon
- Beans
- Carrots
- Asparagus
- Broccoli
- Zucchini
- Celery stalk
- Cucumber
- Bok choy
- Soya beans
- Eggplants
- Peas
- Horseradish

- Olives
- Cauliflower

Meat:
- Beef
- Pork
- Chicken breast
- Sausage
- Lamb

Pantry and condiments:
- Chicken/ beef broth
- Beef/chicken stock
- Almond flour
- Apple cider/balsamic vinegar
- Soy sauce
- Tomato paste
- Coconut flour
- Starch
- Chili sauce

Spices and oils:
- Extra-virgin olive oil
- Cooking spray

- Sesame oil
- Cilantro
- Coriander
- Ginger
- Curry
- Bay leaf
- Basil
- Turmeric
- Sesame seeds
- Cumin
- Garlic

Eggs and dairy:
- Cream
- Eggs
- Cheese
- Butter
- Half and half

Sweeteners:
- Erythritol
- Liquid stevia

Seasoning and flavorings:
- Sage

- Rosemary
- Butter salt
- Tahini
- Miso paste
- Salt
- Oregano
- Paprika
- Parsley
- Onion powder
- Lemon zest/lime juice
- Thyme

Others:

Wine
Mustard
Chives
Almond milk
Coconut milk

Frequently Asked Questions

Below are the answers to some of the most commonly asked questions that should help you clear up some confusion (if you have any).

Why do some foods such as rice, or veggies call for different cooking times in different recipes?

The cooking time does not only depend on the type of ingredient that you are using but on various other factors as well.

When considering vegetables, you have to consider how the veggies are cut. If using a whole cauliflower head, it might be cubed, cut into florets, alternatively, you can have cubed potatoes and whole potatoes.

Cubed variations will always take less time than the whole veggie itself.

The same goes for meat as well, the thickness and the cut largely vary the time taken to cooking the meal properly.

If you are cooking rice, you might be interested to know that pressure cooking rice directly into the pot will cook much faster than pressure cooking the rice in a bowl that is set on the rack.

Is it possible to adjust the temperature of Sautéing or Searing?

Yes, all you have to do is press the Temperature Up and Down arrows twice, and the appliance will change the heat setting and allow you to Saute/Sear at your selected mode.

Is Pre-heating necessary when using the Crisping or Roasting feature?

It is not necessary that you preheat your pot, if you do, you will get better results. Just let the appliance pre-heat for 5 minutes before cooking.

Is it possible to open the lid while cooking?

As long as you are using any of the convection methods such as Air Crisp, Bake/Roast, you are allowed to open the lid at any time you want. Once you open up the lid, the cooking will pause and will only resume once you have securely placed the lid. However, while Pressure Cooking/Steaming, you should never open the lid until the whole cook cycle and pressure release cycle is complete!

Are the different parts of the Foodi Dishwasher safe?

Yes, all the accessories of the Ninja Foodi are dishwasher safe, alongside the inner pot as well. However, keep in mind that the base, Crisping Lid, and Pressure Lid are NOT dishwasher safe and should be cleaned by using a sponge or wet cloth.

How to get rid of the unpleasant smell from the Sealing Ring?

The most basic step to do is to remove the sealing ring after every cook session and washing/drying I before putting it back. You can do this either by hand or by using your dishwasher. If that doesn't do the trick, try to leave it under the sun for a while.